MEMORY MAKERS

Quilted Scrapbooks

Making scrapbook pages with patchwork,
appliqué, and other quilting techniques

SATELLITE PRESS
DENVER, COLORADO

*We dedicate this book to all of our Memory Makers readers whose
beautiful quilt scrapbook pages and ideas are the inspiration on these pages.*

*We extend a special thanks to The Rocky Mountain Quilt Museum of
Golden, Colorado, for making their collection available for this book.*

PROJECT DIRECTORS	Michele & Ron Gerbrandt
EDITORIAL DIRECTOR	Judith Durant
ART DIRECTOR	Sylvie Abecassis
CRAFT DIRECTOR	Pam Klassen
IDEA COORDINATOR	Pennie Stutzman
CRAFT ARTIST	Erikia Ghumm
GRAPHIC DESIGNERS	Bren Frisch, Susha Roberts
PHOTOGRAPHY	Ken Trujillo
ILLUSTRATIONS	Sarah Daniels
CONTRIBUTING ARTISTS	Cynthia Castelluccio, Sarah Fishburn, Pamela Frye, Jennifer T. Johnson, Dawn Mabe, Pam Metzger, Jennifer Pond, Eileen Ruscetta
EDITORIAL SUPPORT	Carolyn Newman, Dena Twinem

MEMORY MAKERS® QUILTED SCRAPBOOKS
Copyright 2000 Satellite Press

Published by Satellite Press
12365 N. Huron Street, Suite 500, Denver, CO 80234
Phone 1-800-366-6465
First edition. Printed in the United States

Library of Congress Cataloging-in-Publication Data

Quilted scrapbooks : making scrapbook pages with patchwork, appliqué,
and other quilting techniques.--1st ed.
    p. cm.
Includes bibliographical references and index.
ISBN 1-89212-710-5 (pbk.)
    1. Photograph albums. 2. Scrapbooks. 3. Paper work. 4. Patchwork. 5. Appliqué I.
Title: At head of title: Memory makers.
TR465.Q.55 2000
745.593--dc21   00-059539

*Distributed to the trade and art markets by
North Light Books, an imprint of F & W Publications, Inc.
1507 Dana Avenue, Cincinnati, OH 45207
1-800-289-0963*

ISBN 1-89212-710-5

*Satellite Press is the home of Memory Makers, the scrapbook magazine dedicated to educating and inspiring scrapbookers.
To subscribe or for more information call 1-800-366-6465. Visit us on the Internet at www.memorymakersmagazine.com*

14

26

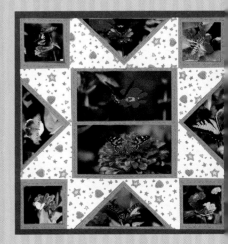

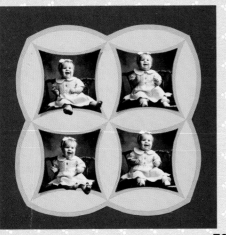

70

52

Contents

Stitching together our memories,
one piece at a time, for years to come.

118

40

56

88

101

109

Introduction

I AM SO EXCITED to be able to present to you this collection of quilted scrapbook page ideas. Ever since the second edition of *Memory Makers* in 1997, when we featured the article "Threads of Memories," I have wanted to further explore the connection between quilting and scrapbooking.

We have divided the book into chapters of quilt patterns or types. For example, there are chapters for stars, samplers, appliqué, and more. Each chapter opens with an actual quilt of the featured type or pattern, and a scrapbook page we created that reflects the design of that quilt. This shows how versatile and inspirational quilt patterns can be when translating to your page. We offer step-by-step instructions and necessary patterns for you to easily create your own page. Each chapter continues on with many diverse page ideas based on the given quilt type. Five pages of templates are included, and two pages of lettering will help you on your way.

What is most exciting to me about this book is that each pattern can be adapted to complement your individual photos. Simply by changing the color of the pattern it can fit your photo theme and color scheme. Just as we have done to the left, Aunt Eliza's Star pattern is shown working with birthday photos, Christmas photos, and baby's first year.

Quilting and scrapbooking have much in common. Scrapbookers can use the same techniques used by quilters, only we crop and mount, rather than cut and sew. Our modern-day crop is like the quilting bees of old. Women gather together to share friendship, ideas and support, and to trade little bits of treasured scraps. We hope the ideas and methods presented here will inspire your own quilted scrapbooks.

Michele

As shown at left, the same motif takes on completely different looks when made with different photographs and in different colored papers.
See page 127 for paper details.

Basic Tools and Supplies

PENS AND MARKERS Use pigment pens and markers for journaling as well as creating stitching lines on your quilt pages. Pens and markers should be fade-resistant, waterproof, and colorfast.

ADHESIVES Many glues are considered permanent, such as the dry adhesive, double-sided tape, and photo splits shown here. "Two-way glues" allow you to move a photo after placement. Be sure the adhesive you choose is acid free.

RULERS A straight ruler is necessary for cutting straight lines with a craft knife. Use fancy rulers for borders and embellishments.

SCISSORS Use straight sharp scissors to cut intricate shapes that you can't cut with a craft knife. Use decorative scissors for mats and special effects.

PAGE PROTECTORS These are plastic sleeves made to fit over album pages. Make sure the plastic does not contain PVC (polyvinyl chloride).

PAPER For both backgrounds and embellishments, we recommend the use of archival quality, photo-safe paper and other supplies for your scrapbooks.

TEMPLATES There are dozens of quilt templates readily available. These are either positive or negative patterns and are made especially for the scrapbooker or quilter.

CRAFT KNIFE AND CUTTING MAT For the most accurate results when cutting straight lines, use a craft knife, ruler and cutting mat.

Working with Templates

Using Positive Templates

To use a positive template, simply trace around the outside edges onto your chosen paper. Then cut along the drawn line. Because you can't see what's behind these templates, they work best for plain paper or when it doesn't matter too much what part of a printed paper you're going to use.

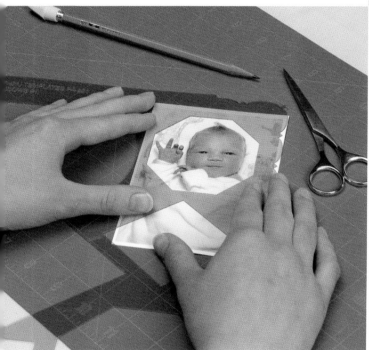

Using Negative Templates

A negative template is one where the shape has been cut out of the middle of a piece of paper or plastic. These templates allow you to see exactly what your finished shape will look like. Use these when cropping photos or looking for a specific pattern in a printed paper—you can move a negative template around until you get just the portion of photo or paper you want.

Making Your Own Templates

Quilt books are teeming with patterns that the scrapbooker can make into templates for use with paper. The patterns usually have two outlines—a cutting line is the outside edge and a sewing line is inside the cutting line. Since we do not need seam allowances for paper quilts, you will cut along the sewing line.

Using a light board or tracing paper, trace along the sewing line of the design. Cut the design out with sharp scissors. Now you can trace around this pattern onto stencil film (Grafix) for a see-through template or onto cardstock or other sturdy material. Once the pattern is on the cardstock, you may choose to cut out a positive or a negative template. If the template material is opaque, a negative template will allow you to choose a specific pattern in your paper or a particular portion of your photograph.

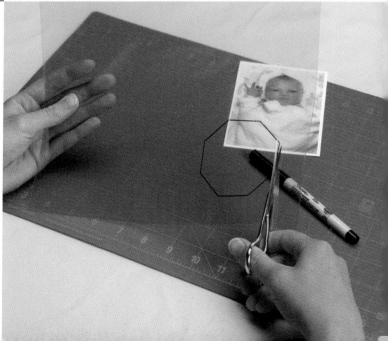

Choosing Colors and Papers

The most important thing to consider when choosing colors is whether or not they complement your photographs. All of the quilt designs you'll find in this book can be done in any color scheme you choose—from bright primaries to soft pastels. The effects will be different, but all are valid choices.

Many quilts typically use multiple colors and prints, and there are thousands of papers to choose from. In general, since the individual pieces of your quilted scrapbook page will be small, it's best to choose a small print. If the print is too large, it will be lost when cut into a ¼" or smaller piece. The other thing to consider is whether or not your contrasting papers will show off the lines of your design to best advantage. To illustrate these concepts, we've made three pages using the same photographs and the same quilt design but different paper colors.

A Good Choice

This page is done with a monochromatic blue-gray color scheme, in prints and solids, ranging from dark to medium to light tones. The colors go well with the photographs, particularly with the stony shore. However, when these colors are combined to form the star motif, some of the definition is lost. The two medium toned papers are so similar that you can't distinguish one from the other, and the overall design of the page looks like a large X.

A Better Choice

For this page we chose a dark and a medium blue, a medium green, and black. Again, the colors go well with the photographs, picking up details found in them. This page is more successful at delineating the star pattern because the individual shapes in each of the blocks contrast with the one next to it. And while the medium blue and medium green are very similar in tone, they are more distinguishable than the two blue-grays in the previous example because they are different colors.

Located on the island of Mon, in the south of Denmark are the cliffs of Mon. These chalk cliffs Rise hundreds of feet from the sea, and are extremely beautiful from top and bottom. My last month in Denmark, my family took me on a nature walk on the cliffs. It took 500 steps to get to the base of the cliffs, and to view their magnificence from the shale and flint covered beach below. Jørgen and I searched for petrified octopus on our walk. It was so much fun, and nature at its finest!

The Best Solution

This example is the most successful of the three. Once again, the colors go well with the photographs, picking up even more of the details than the previous examples. And the four colors used in the corner blocks offer more contrast than the other two pages, making the star quilt motif very obvious. Notice how the light blocks in the corners really help the star pattern show well.

Adapting Designs to Fit Your Page

Adapting or creating a design to fit different page sizes is not difficult; it just takes planning. Although you will not be able to exactly duplicate a 12 x 12" page to fit your 8½ x 11" book (one is square while the other is rectangular), you can use one of the following techniques to duplicate the essence of a design to fit any page. Downsizing is a bit trickier than upsizing, but both can be accomplished with great results.

Adapting with Borders

Using borders is an easy way to adapt a design, especially if you're upsizing. The 8½ x 11" page shown above, based on a simple nine patch quilt, consists of an 8½ x 8½" quilt block with a 2½" border at the bottom. We can exactly reproduce this design (using the same size photographs) on a 12 x 12" page. Simply center the 8½ x 8½" quilt block on the page and add a 1¾" border to the top, bottom, and each side. Alternatively, if you have the ability to resize your photographs, you could make this design fill the page by combining nine 4" squares.

But what if you see a 12 x 12" page design that you want to use in your 8½ x 11" book? To adapt the design using borders, you can make the design into a two-page spread. Then you can simply add 2½" borders to the outsides of both pages to complete the design. We chose to make these borders with photographs.

Changing the Layout

Many quilt designs can be adapted to fit any page. Here is the same basic octagon design shown on a 3½ x 5" spiral-bound page, a rectangular 8½ x 11" page, and a square 12 x 12" page. For the 3½ x 5" page, the octagons are smallest, slightly larger for the 8½ x 11" page, and largest for the 12 x 12" page. You can get the various sizes by ordering smaller or larger prints or by cropping differently.

Squares and Rectangles

Quilts of simple squares and rectangles have been plentiful throughout history. Made from scraps, these quilts were affordable, often comprised of fabric on hand rather than specially purchased.

The Log Cabin is a popular design that begins with one square in the center around which strips or long narrow rectangles are built. Many Log Cabin quilts begin with a red square in the center, which symbolizes the hearth of the home. Using strips of printed and plain papers, this design is ideal for a scrapbook page of any size.

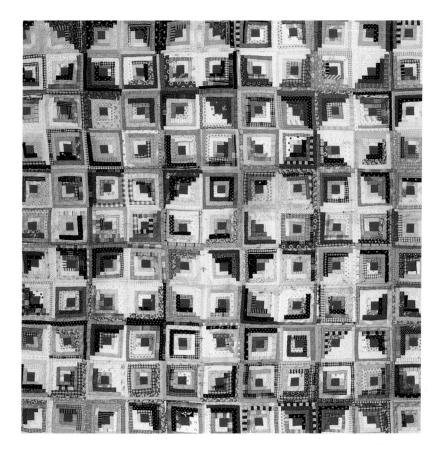

Log Cabin This quilt was donated to the Rocky Mountain Quilt Museum by Ella Appel of Boulder, Colorado. The fabric dates the quilt's creation to around 1880. From the collection of the Rocky Mountain Quilt Museum. 1996.2.6.

Log Cabin

THE BASIC BLOCK IS CALLED THE SPIRALING LOG CABIN. Four blocks are put together for this page, which features a photograph of, what else, lumberjacks. The diagonal split in shading is achieved by using darker prints on one half of the block and lighter prints on the other. You will need equal amounts of light and dark prints. Following the diagram for each block, add strips of light and dark papers, building out to the edges of your page.

Debra Fee, Broomfield, Colorado

Supplies needed

8 dark printed papers, 8 light printed papers and red solid paper, black and white paper for photo mat.

1. *Cut 32 light and 32 dark ¹/₂" printed paper strips. (See page 127 for paper sources.) You may do this with a ruler and craft knife or you may mark your paper with a pencil and cut with scissors. The important thing is to be accurate and consistent. (Figures 1 and 2.)*
2. *Divide page into four quarters and mark with pencil.*
3. *Following diagram for light and dark strips, glue strips down starting with an inside corner. Work one quarter of the page at a time. (Figure 3.)*
4. *Cut four 2" red squares and glue one to the center of each block.*
5. *Crop and double mat photo with black and white paper, leaving very narrow mats so as not to detract from the quilt.*
6. *Write journal entries in the center squares.*

To make an 8¹/₂ x 11" page *Proceed as described above with the following exceptions: Use 6 vertical strips (3 each of light and dark) and 8 horizontal strips (4 each of light and dark) for each block—this will make rectangular rather than square blocks. Cut 1¹/₂ x 1¹/₂" red centers for each block. See pages 12 and 13 for more ideas on resizing.*

Ann Thatcher Griffith

BUILD A CABIN OF PHOTOS

This simple page, based on the Log Cabin quilt, is made with school and family portraits. The ⅜"-wide red logs are cut from printed paper (Keeping Memories Alive), and the font is Dimples Fun Font (Karen Foster Design).

Joy Candrian, Sandy, Utah

VARIATIONS OF THE LOG CABIN

pattern are made by different arrangements of light and dark strips. Some resulting patterns have names such as Barn Raising, Old-Fashioned Log Cabin, and Courthouse Steps.

Summer Swimmer

COLOR COPY FABRICS FOR A LOG CABIN QUILT

When Geraldine visited her aunt Marie-Dominique, she was introduced to scrapbooking and made sixty of her own pages in three weeks! Marie-Dominique used a photocopying technique, a trick she learned from her friend Michele Brock Fischer, to create this page. Marie-Dominique photocopied traditional French fabrics onto acid-free paper, creating a collection of custom-made scrapbooking paper. The cool Provençal prints make a wonderful frame for "swimming Geraldine."

Marie-Dominique Giraud, Lyon, France

A Day in the Forest

MAKE PATCHES WITH DIE CUTS

Kimberly used die cut blocks (Accu-Cut) and assembled them into a classic nine-patch quilt design. The corners of the blocks converge to create flower-like motifs in the borders, and Kimberly cropped her photos with indented curved edges to add dimension to the blocks. The use of both plain and printed paper (Provo Craft) creates more visual appeal.

Kimberly Ussery, Palm Desert, California

Chimney Rock Park

LOOK THROUGH THE ATTIC WINDOW

The Attic Window quilt block makes a wonderful frame for photographs of any subject. Simply cutting one end of each paper rectangle at an angle creates a 3D effect—it's as if you are actually looking at these photographs through a window. Cut strips of wood and gold paper (Hot Off the Press) using the template on page 122 and arrange them around 2½" square photos as shown. "Button" it up with red circles punched with a ⅝" circle punch (Family Treasures) embellished with hand-drawn holes and stitches.

Brenda Raines, Lumberport, West Virginia

Punch Art

PUNCH ART IS EASY All you need are a few punches and some paper to create captivating art from simple, punched paper shapes. Punch art adds charm and whimsy to your scrapbook pages. It can also extend your budget by making good use of paper scraps that might otherwise be thrown away. Use additional designs like those shown at right as border squares to brighten any page. All designs were created using a simple ⅜" square punch.

Autumn

PUNCH QUILT BLOCKS IN FALL COLORS

Kathleen has created six different quilt blocks, all using only three colors of paper and one square punch!

Kathleen Fritz, St. Charles, Missouri

1. *Punch 17 yellow squares, 17 orange squares, and 16 green squares.*
2. *Cut 2 yellow squares diagonally in half and 4 yellow squares diagonally in quarters.*
3. *Cut 4 orange squares diagonally in half and 3 orange squares diagonally in quarters.*
4. *Cut 2 green squares diagonally in half and 4 green squares diagonally in quarters.*
5. *Assemble quilt blocks as shown and mount to page.*

A Quilt of Love

EMBOSS SOME YELLOW RIBBONS

Parchment paper, gingham, and solids combine to create this variation on the nine-patch quilt comprised of 2½" squares. To highlight the yellow ribbon hostage theme of the page, Shari used a stencil (Plaid) to emboss ribbons in the yellow squares (see page 110 for embossing techniques). Use a pen to decoratively "stitch" the plain squares.

Shari Dinnen, Mount Dora, Florida

Quilt From a Stencil

Heidi is always looking for new page ideas, and a Stens-a-Quilt template (Classic Trio) solved her problem for this page. Simply trace the negative stencil shape onto paper or photo and carefully cut the image out with scissors. Then use the outside part of the stencil to create borders.

Heidi Bamber, Vista, California

Noah's Ark Puff Quilt
TIE UP A PATCHWORK PAGE

Jenny made a quilt for her baby's room and used leftover material as part of the layout of this commemorative page. She cut ten 2½" squares and a heart, placed them over batting, tied them together, and glued them to the page. She also added a button to the heart. The photos are double-mounted with white and blue paper, and the journaling is done with Crayon font (DJ Inkers).

Jennifer Blackham, West Jordan, Utah

A Close-Knit Group
JOURNAL A FRIENDSHIP QUILT

When Michelle announced she was relocating and had to leave her job, Judy gave each of their co-workers a piece of acid-free white paper on which to write farewell wishes. Judy then pieced together this quilt, matching the wishes with photographs of the wish makers taken at various work events. Twelve 3" squares comprise the border, and the center "square" is 4" and flanked with triangles made from two 3" squares cut diagonally in half. Printed papers (The Paper Patch) and "stitching" with pens complete the look.

Judy Iverson, Flower Mound, Texas

AN OLD WORLD TRADITION

held that a young woman must prepare far in advance the quilts for the home she would make once she married. A maiden pieced many squares, made covers, and stored them until she found the man she would marry. She would presumably then quilt them once in her new home.

In America, quilting parties were common. The party at which the bride-to-be brought out her pieced covers was the time for the engagement announcement. The neighbors then quilted for the happy couple.

Quilts for Kosovo

IN JUNE OF 1999, Samantha's school art teacher did a project with the entire School Street School to make quilts for Kosovo refugees. Sabina helped out by cutting the 8 x 8" squares and sewing them together for the children to then tie.

James and Samantha both made quilts for Kosovo refugees and included their messages of friendship on the backside of their quilts. They did a wonderful job!

Sabina Dougherty-Wiebkin, Lebanon, New Hampshire

Heritage Album Page
CREATE A QUILT WITH TINTYPES

(UPPER RIGHT) Debra chose muted colors for the 2½" squares that complement the old photographs and tintypes she used in her heritage album. Using an oval template (Creative Memories) to crop the photograph makes it really stand out on the square patchwork background. The adhesive photo corners (K & Company) also add to the heritage look. Use a banner sticker (Frances Meyer) for the title and brown pen for journaling and "stitches."

Debra Fee, Broomfield, Colorado

Penn's Colony Festival
QUILT A COMPLEMENTARY BORDER

(FAR UPPER RIGHT) Jeannie made borders for this scrapbook page that mimic the border in the quilt the Economy Junior Women's Club raffled off. The 2"-wide border is made from 1½" squares of mauve, burgundy, dark green, cream, denim blue, and navy blue. Triangles are made by cutting squares diagonally in half. The ends are filled in with two ⅝" burgundy squares, halved. A cutout from a promotional page adds context, and the pen "stitching" holds it all together.

Jeannie Smith, Baden, Pennsylvania

Remembering Grandfather
ADD FINISHING TOUCH WITH A BORDER

(LOWER RIGHT) This simple border created with printed hydrangea paper (Hot Off the Press) turns a plain page into a quilt page. The 1" squares are used whole and halved and are outlined with pen "stitching." Joy gave the digital photos a slight plum tint, which she then accentuated with a colored paper background. The newspaper clipping was scanned from the original and journaling was done with a computer font.

Joy Carey, Visalia, California

Quilt Album Title Page
SPECIAL EFFECTS WITH HIGH-CONTRAST PAPERS

(FAR LOWER RIGHT) This simple quilt motif, a variation of one called Grandmother's Choice, makes a nice title page for a quilt or heritage album. The high contrast of black against beige is quite dramatic.

Sharon Murray, Bozeman, Montana

THE OVERALL PATTERN *of many quilts is imperfect—some blocks are light where they should be dark. Often a quilt-maker would deliberately break the pattern in order to avoid inviting disaster for trying to imitate God's perfect work, a superstition that is still adhered to. When you come across a perfectly symmetrical design with one obvious flaw, this is the reason.*

Ina Belle Hatch and Clyde Elwood Barkdull married November 2, 1910 in Grand Rapids, MI

Samuel and Amanda Bear Specks

The Specks's Restaurant (Owned by Sam & Amanda)

The Frank Bear Home in Indiana

Our family is like a patchwork quilt
With kindness gently sewn
Each piece is an original
With beauty all its own
With threads of warmth and happiness
It's tightly stitched together
To last in love throughout the years
Our family is forever

Our Family Quilt

QUILT WITH PRE-PRINTED PAPER

(UPPER LEFT) Kandi had photographs left at the end of the year, so she decided to make this simple patchwork quilt to use them. She simply mounted a photo in every other 2¼" square of pre-printed square patchwork paper (Frances Meyer). She then wrote the months of the year on colored scraps of paper and added one to each photo.

Kandi Madden, Erie, Colorado

Bunny Quilt

MAKE A PATCHWORK POCKET

(UPPER RIGHT) Mario got a bunny booklet at preschool, and it inspired his mom to make this bunny quilt page. She put Mario's picture on the bunny marker and stores it "behind the bushes." The 4" squares of green and yellow paper are joined at the corners with ⅜" hot pink squares. Add "stitching" with a white pen.

Linda Strauss, Provo, Utah

Pretty Patchwork of Spring

TEAR A PAPER QUILT

(LOWER LEFT) Linda got the idea for this page from a piece of pre-printed paper she saw at her local scrapbook store. She decided to make the page by tearing different colored paper into 2½ x 3" quilt blocks. She chose colors that complement the photos, which works to highlight the subjects and capture the feeling of spring.

Linda Beardsley, Tokyo, Japan

SABRINA
SARAH
MEADS

SEPT. 26
1999

7:53AM

6LB 15OZ
18 3/4"

Cari

FILL A QUILT WITH SILHOUETTES

(PREVIOUS PAGE, LOWER RIGHT) Cindy's daughter is now 15, so these pictures are old (and irreplaceable). When they were taken, cameras weren't as advanced as they are today, so zooming in wasn't an option. Cindy silhouetted her photos and filled a quilt page with them. She used gingham and polka dot papers (Creative Memories) and letter and accent stickers (Mrs. Grossman's).

Cindy Hodge, Lincoln, Nebraska

Birth Announcement Page

BUTTON IT UP

(ABOVE) The inspiration for this page came from Sabrina's baby blanket. Michelle made the paper—she designed her own patterns and printed the outlines on her inkjet printer, then used colored pencils to fill in the designs. Satin ribbon makes borders and buttons are punched. To create "embroidered" journaling, Michelle sketched with pencil then went over that with a gel pen in a zigzag motion.

Michelle Meads, Fort Lauderdale, Florida

Star Patchwork

One of the most beautiful, versatile, and frequently used motifs for quilts is the star. Inspired from nature, there are many variations of star quilts including Texas Star, Feather Star, Star of Bethlehem, and Ohio Star, shown here. Because the design comprises squares and a simple triangle, the Ohio Star can be easily incorporated into scrapbook pages—the cutting and alignment of these basic shapes is a breeze with paper!

Ohio Star This quilt was made by Jo Ann Morgan of Littleton, Colorado. It was made during the 1990s using new fabrics printed with traditional designs from the 30s and 40s. Courtesy of Jo Ann Morgan.

Ohio Star

THE OHIO STAR is simple to construct—it uses only squares and triangles. The most logical way to use this motif for a page is to copy one star block. Simply divide your page into nine equal squares—four squares are then divided into four equal triangles. Take the opportunity this design provides to add a photo in the center and one in each of the four corners.

Marilyn Garner, San Diego, California

Supplies needed
*1 light printed paper and
1 dark contrast paper.*

1. *Measure and cut two 4" squares of dark paper. (Figure 1.)*
2. *Cut each square diagonally twice. You now have eight equal triangles. (Figure 2.)*
3. *Arrange and adhere triangles to page. (Figure 3.)*
4. *Crop one 4 x 4" photo for the center and four 2¾" squares for the corners. Crop corner photos diagonally. (For best results, use a clear template for the cropping photos. See Working with Templates on page 9 for more information.) Adhere to page.*
5. *Add "stitching" and journaling. Marilyn used a sun punch for zeros to add shine to her title.*

To make an 8½ x 11" page *Mark off the top 2½" of the page and use it for a title, border, or journaling. Alternatively, you could mark off a 1¼" border at the top and bottom of the page. This leaves an 8½ x 8½" block. Proceed as described above, but begin with two 2¹⁵⁄₁₆" squares. Your center photo will be 2¹⁵⁄₁₆" square, and corner photos will be 1⁷⁄₁₆" squares. See page 33 for an example and pages 12 and 13 for more ideas on resizing.*

My Grandma

JOURNAL A TRIBUTE

Although this quilt design (Aunt Addie's Album) incorporates different sized triangles, they all begin as squares. You'll need two 5" squares of pale green (one cut in square quarters), and 3½" squares as follows: two pale green, halved diagonally; one each of polka dot (The Paper Patch) and floral (MiniGraphics) paper, each cut in square quarters, then each quarter is diagonally halved. Theresa matted her photo with the dark green background paper and journaled her grandmother's loves with a complementary green pen.

Theresa Lindamood, Sacramento, California

Star with Butterflies

CREATE A SHOWCASE FOR THEME PHOTOS

Lisa loves photographing the butterflies in her garden, and this quilt page shows them off to great advantage. Lisa started with a piece of 12 x 12" paper for the background, and a 6 x 6" printed piece for the star. The printed paper (NRN Designs) is quartered, then diagonally halved to make 8 triangles, and the tips of the triangles are trimmed to fit the page. "Stitching" is added on the blue background, and a darker blue border is added with ⅜" paper strips.

Lisa Laird, Orange City, Iowa

STAR LIGHT, STAR BRIGHT

Some variation of the diamond or square forms the base of all star patterns, which far outnumber all other designs. The simplest form is an eight-pointed star known as the "Star-of-LeMoyne." This is of French origin. The LeMoyne brothers were given a grant of land in 1699 known as Louisiana, and in 1718 they founded the city of New Orleans. In the New England states the name was shortened to "Lemon Star." —From The Romance of the Patchwork Quilt in America *by Carrie A. Hall and Rose G. Kretsinger.*

The Lemon Star is an eight-pointed star similar to the one shown at right, except that the points are two-toned or alternating light and dark.

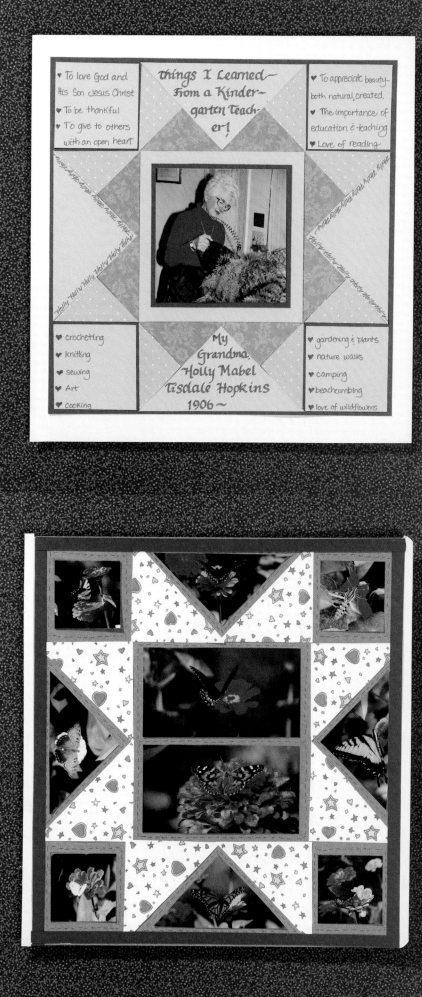

Family Reunion Quilt

MAKE YOUR OWN PAPER BY SCANNING FABRIC

Carol's sister made a memory quilt with wedding pictures of the preceding generation, and she finished just in time for the family reunion. She scanned one of the blocks and two of the fabrics and Carol used them to create blocks for journaling. She journaled with a computer font and printed the blocks on her color printer. Shown here is one page of a two-page spread that has $2\frac{3}{8}$" blocks mounted on a plain blue background.

Carol Thomson, Oyama, British Columbia

Our Family Heritage

QUILT A TITLE PAGE

Stephanie makes a title page for all her albums. This dramatic page is made with eight 2" squares of red paper, six 1" squares of navy paper, and four 1 x 10" strips of cream paper. Create triangles by cutting squares in half and arrange all pieces on a white background. Print your title in a Vivaldi font and trace it in pen using a light table.

Stephanie West, Spring Valley, California

Pull-up Pocket Page

JILL CHOSE GREEN AND BLUE paper to match the colors in her family's Christmas outfits. The star is assembled with 3¾" squares using gingham and plaid (The Paper Patch) papers, and the top of the star keeps a special note about that particular Christmas. You see, the family all caught the flu. Jill didn't think everyone who looks through her book would want the details, so she pocketed them.

Jill Gross, Roselle, Illinois

1. *Cut 3¾" squares as follows: 4 plaid, 4 gingham, and 5 polka dot.*
   - *Alternately mount the polka dot and plaid squares onto solid background in 9-patch pattern as shown.*
   - *On the back, use a pencil and ruler to divide gingham squares diagonally into quarters. Cut one triangle from each square.*
   - *Adhere the gingham squares to the plaid squares as shown, making sure you glue only the very edges of the sides and bottom of the top part of the star. (Figure 1.)*
2. *Cut a piece of plain white paper 3¼ x 3½". Journal on the white paper and insert into top of star. (Figure 2.) Make sure the message is hidden when the paper is inserted into the pocket.*
3. *Punch a medium star from yellow paper and adhere to pocket. (Figure 3.)*

These Are the Special Times

PIECE A CHRISTMAS TITLE PAGE

Cherie named this page after the title track from Celine Dion's Christmas CD, which is appropriate to her feelings about Christmas with family. The journaling is done on a computer with a fancy font. The triangles are cut from 2½" squares of printed paper (Keeping Memories Alive) and complement the cream squares (Pebbles in My Pocket). The overall size of each square is 3½".

Cherie Thierman, Fairview, Pennsylvania

Stitched with Smiles

USE LETTERING TO ACCENT YOUR THEME

The title lettering is traced from a fancy lettering book and is only one of many possibilities for use on a quilt page. Patterned paper and "stitching" complete the look. The stars on the "stitched" page are made with triangles from 3" squares and the "smiles" page uses 1¼" squares.

Kelly Leppink, Lakeview, Michigan

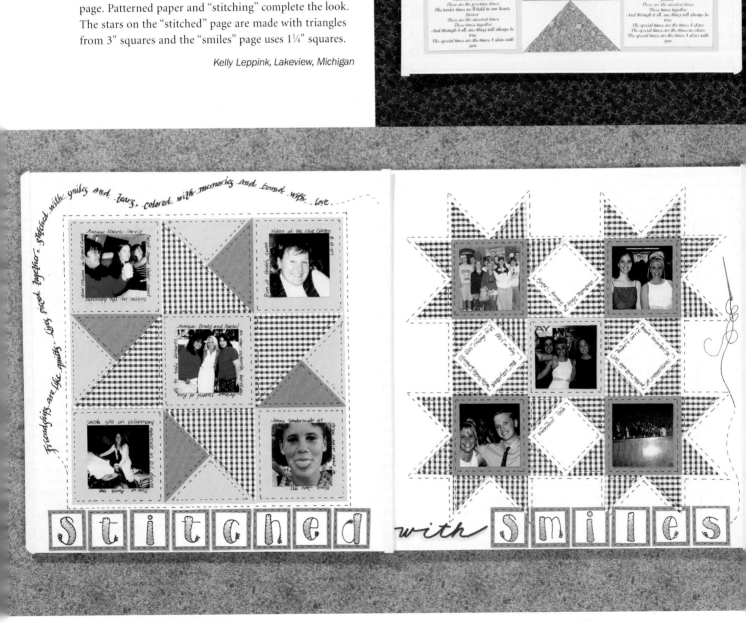

Sorority Quilt

STITCH TOGETHER DOZENS OF SMALL PHOTOS

Jill loves making quilt pages, and for these photos from a sorority event she chose pink and green, the colors of Delta Zeta. The triangles are cut from 2⅝" squares, and the small pink squares and photos are ⅞". Journaling is done in small lettering around the outside of the page so as not to detract from the quilt block. Letters cut from plaid paper and stitching add the finishing touch.

Jill Gross, Roselle, Illinois

A Patchwork of Love

FIT A SQUARE BLOCK ON A RECTANGULAR PAGE

Just because quilt blocks are square is no reason not to use them on your 8½ x 11" page. Shari simply made her star block 8 x 8" and ran a large title block across the top.

Shari Dinnen, Mountt Dora, Florida

Quilt Raffle, A Family Affair

ON CHRISTMAS DAY, my grandmother had each of her five daughters draw numbers for quilts that she had been working on for years. My mother was in pursuit of one quilt in particular. She even had a deal with one of her sisters to trade if she got the prized piece. But when she opened her package and found it was not the quilt she was after, she was not disappointed. She cried tears of joy—the quilt was beautiful and, best of all, her mother handcrafted it.

—Kimberly Smith, Lakeland, Florida

Peel and Stick a Quilt

Making an Ohio Star scrapbook page couldn't be easier with Create-a-Quilt (Pamela Shoy Papers). This product features pre-cut peel and stick paper shapes in a variety of colors. Here we've used lime green from the kit and coordinated it with a green gingham paper (Design Originals). Each kit comes with tips on using the shapes for a variety of scrapbook page sizes.

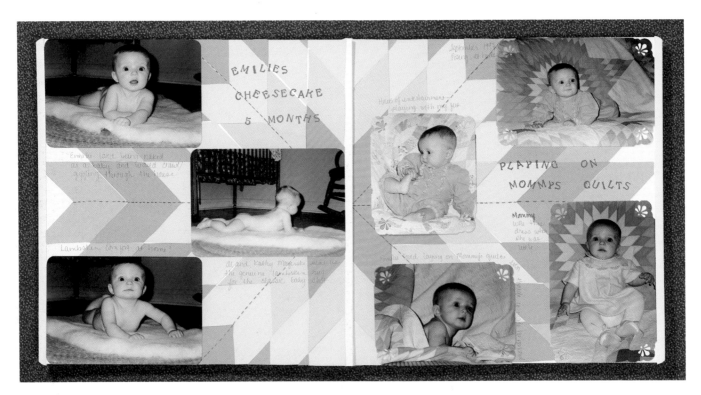

Emilie's Cheesecake

QUILT A PAGE TO MIMIC THE PHOTOS

Robin used the Lone Star quilt design from the quilt in a photo of Emilie to create the star background for this page. It is very easily pieced together with 68 two-inch diamonds (template on page 122) in five playful colors. Some photos are punched (Family Treasures) in the corners for added interest. Journal right on the "quilt," add photos and title with rubber stamps (Hero Arts).

Robin Nordhues, Minneapolis, Minnesota

Radiant Star Quilt
MAKE A CLASSIC FROM THE 1870S

This page is patterned after the Feathered Star, a quilt block from the late nineteenth century. This is a great design for using up lots of photos. Using the templates on page 123, crop eight cone-shaped photos, sixteen triangles, plus sixteen 1" squares (halve eight of these squares for triangles) and one large photo for center of page. Arrange as shown and outline with $\frac{1}{16}$" strips of paper. The background paper (Close to My Heart) is accented with small star punches and alphabet punches (Family Treasures).

Rita Brei, Mission Viejo, California

Autumn Beauty
RECORD A STUNNING FOLIAGE

There is no worry about choosing the right colors when nature does the work for you! Karen simply cropped her wonderful fall photos taken at Lake of the Ozarks using a diamond-shaped template (Creative Memories) and pieced them together on a skylike background (Geographics).

Karen Krone, Florissant, Missouri

A Day at the Beach
SCRAP QUILT WITH BLACK AND WHITE PHOTOS

Stacy used bright colors and interesting textures to complement her black and white beach photos. The bright gold starburst in the center symbolizes the sun. You'll need two 2¼" squares in gold for the center, four 2¼" squares in dark blue, and two 3" squares of printed paper (Provo Craft). The border is made with ½" strips, and the corners are from ½" squares.

Stacy McFadden, Kingwood, Texas

Blazing Star Quilt

Eight blue and ten red simple diamonds are built around a star center (templates on page 126)
for this special Christmas page starring Anna and Michael. Blue squares of 1⅜" and 1⅞"
are used to make the triangles. Assemble the pieces as shown and outline with ⅛" strips of green vellum (The Paper Company).
Crop photos to fit and trim page with ⅛" strips of blue paper. Rita used printed paper (The Paper Company) at the star tips and
accented her page with snowflake and alphabet punches (Family Treasures) and added "stitching" with a metallic pen.

Rita Brei, Mission Viejo, California

Christmas Social

MAKE A STAR OF YOUR FRIENDS

The Texas Star quilt pattern makes good use of small images. Solid-color mounting paper makes this a spectacular page—in this case of a girl's night out Christmas Party. Crop ten photos and assemble around center star (template on page 123). Red trimming is ⅜" wide.

Sandra de St. Croix, St. Albert, Alberta

Family Reunion

PIECE A SIX-POINTED STAR

All of Joy's six family photographs have at least one thing in common—the color red. What better way to accentuate this than with a red and white star motif? Using a template stencil (Creative Memories), cut diamond shapes of plain and gingham paper and of photographs. Arrange as shown.

Joy Carey, Visalia, California

Thanksgiving in New England

REMEMBER A TRAVELING VACATION

The stars are made with a diamonds (see template on page 126) of photographs and gingham paper. Ports of call are journaled in hearts and around the stars and then "stitched" to the page.

Michelle Robblee, Newcastle, Washington

A Quilter's Album

Sally has been an avid quilter for more than twelve years. It wasn't long after she began scrapbooking that Sally began making "quilts" on her scrapbook pages. She'd seen some quilt pages done, but none that incorporated actual quilt patterns. And that's just what she's done on these pages, which are but a small sampling of those she's made. And all the patterned papers that are now readily available make scrapbook quilting more fun than ever.

Sally found quilt patterns that she likes in her many quilt books and used them for cutting paper for her pages. Shown here clockwise from right are the Variable Star, Flying Geese, Grandmother's Flower Garden, the Ohio Star, and the Kansas Star. Sally "stitches" all of her quilts with a black pen, and sometimes incorporates plain white blocks for journaling, such as in Flying Geese and the Ohio Star.

Sally Swift, Jacksonville, Florida

VARIABLE STAR

KANSAS STAR

I will keep Christmas in my heart all year.

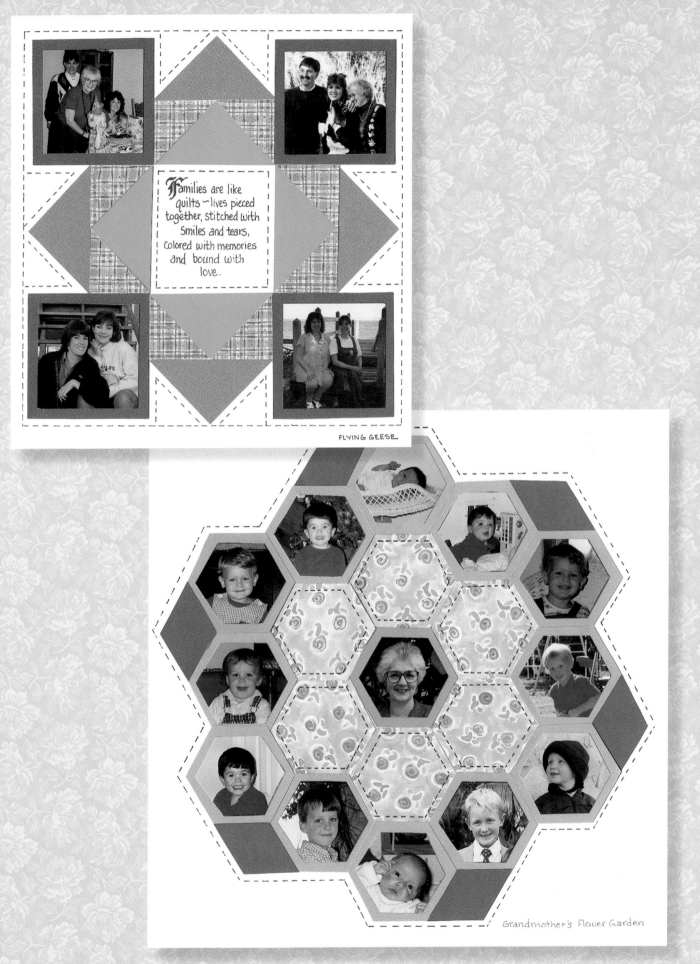

Families are like quilts — lives pieced together, stitched with smiles and tears, colored with memories and bound with love.

FLYING GEESE

Grandmother's Flower Garden

MAGGIE
July 10, 1983

Hexagons and Octagons

Hexagons and octagons are among the most popular geometric shapes used in pieced quilts. When an octagon or hexagon is used in a one-patch design, it being the only shape in a quilt, the resulting quilts are called Grandmother's Flower Garden (as shown here), Honeycomb, or Mosaics, depending on the colors used and the arrangement of the pieces.

Because at least two of the sides are cut on the bias, these quilts are tricky to make in fabric. But with paper, all you need is precise cutting for success.

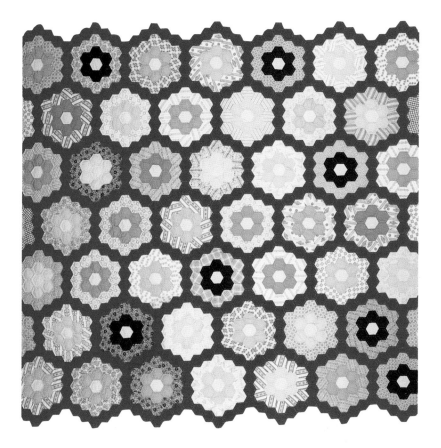

Grandmother's Flower Garden Eugenia Mitchell, founder of the Rocky Mountain Quilt Museum, obtained the top of this quilt from Betty Maxwell. Eugenia completed the quilt in 1977. From the collection of the Rocky Mountain Quilt Museum. 1991.1.19.

Grandmother's Flower Garden

THIS PAGE WAS MADE USING an actual quilting hexagon template that was reduced on a copy machine until it was just the right size for the page. Precise cutting is essential so that your pieces will line up correctly. When making a page like this one, use small prints for the little shapes, and the smaller your pieces, the smaller your "stitches" should be.

Debra Fee, Broomfield, Colorado

Supplies needed

Hexagon patterns (page 126), 2 dark solid papers, 5 medium toned printed papers, 5 medium toned solid papers.

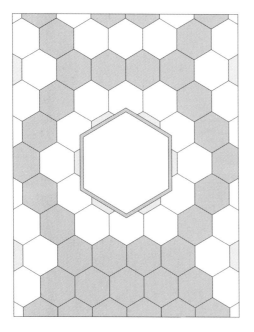

1. *Make a template of the large hexagon (see page 126), and use it to crop photo. Make a mat for the photo by cutting a slightly larger shape from plain paper. Make a template from the small hexagon pattern. (Figure 1.)*
2. *Cut small hexagon pieces for this page as follows: 6 dark blue, 9 blue plaid, 4 each of 4 other prints, 6 solids for centers. (Figure 2. See page 127 for paper sources.)*
3. *Mark the center of your page. Working from the center out, assemble hexagons as shown. Use dark red paper as the background of the page and use the template to draw these hexagons with a pen rather than cut them out. When you get to the edges, use partial shapes to fill the page. (Figure 3.)*
4. *Add stitching detail with a fine point pen.*
5. *Mount photo and add journaling. This title was done with letter stickers (Frances Meyer).*

To make a 12 x 12" page *Proceed as described above, adding more hexagons as necessary to fill the page. See pages 12 and 13 for more ideas on resizing.*

If Friends Were Flowers...

PLANT A PASTEL GARDEN

With a little bit of planning, sophisticated pages such as this one are simple to make. Melinda used coordinating printed papers (Keeping Memories Alive), a birch leaf punch (Family Treasures), and an octagon nested template (Provo Craft). Decorative "stitching" is added with pen.

Melinda Elliott, Johnson City, Tennessee

Grandma's Garden of Love

RESIZE PHOTOS TO FIT

Darlene scanned photographs of her mother's grandchildren and printed them out just the right size for this classic quilt pattern. She cut hexagons (template on page 126) of the photos and printed papers (The Paper Patch), then strategically mounted them on a solid background; she then penned in the rest of the pieces. The title is printed from a computer onto vellum.

Darlene Bruehl, Dayton, Tennessee

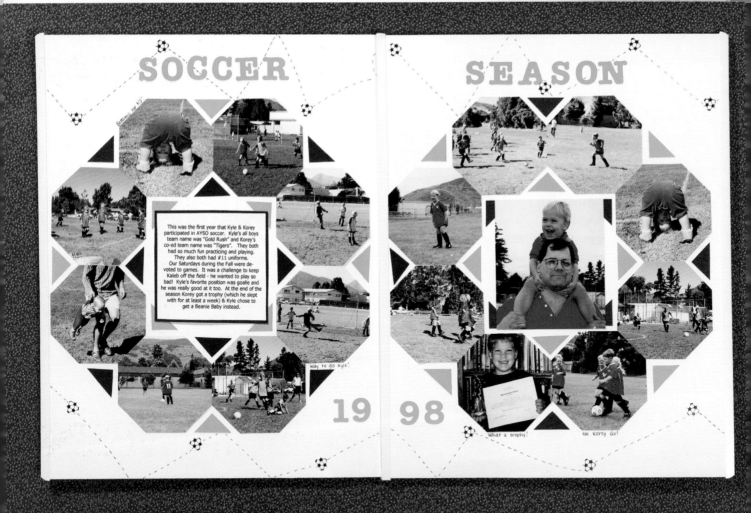

SOCCER SEASON

This was the first year that Kyle & Korey participated in AYSO soccer. Kyle's all boys team name was "Gold Rush" and Korey's co-ed team name was "Tigers". They both had so much fun practicing and playing. They also both had #11 uniforms. Our Saturdays during the Fall were devoted to games. It was a challenge to keep Kaleb off the field - he wanted to play so bad! Kyle's favorite position was goalie and he was really good at it too. At the end of the season Korey got a trophy (which he slept with for at least a week) & Kyle chose to get a Beanie Baby instead.

19 98

Way to go Kyle!

What a trophy!

Go Korey Go!

Bees
Yellow, Black
gather dusty pollen
busy workers
Bees

honey comb
sticky
golden
treat
Sweet nectar

FOR SALE
MID-LAND EXECUTIVE 1 REALTORS
517-839-9655

From the Homestead (Mt. Vernon, Ohio) to the Haven (Midland, Michigan)

Nana and Papa preparing to build on Lot 13 Winterberry Ct.

Nate and Colin love to visit the site of the home, especially when they get to sit in a truck!

"Hey, where are Nana and Papa?" That was Nate's question when we first visited "where Nana & Papa will live."

With almost daily drive-by trips, we eagerly watched as the house began to take shape.

Nate & Colin played in the sand as the builders worked. What could be more fun than watching the crews?!

The boys were thrilled to "hide" in the closets and run from empty room to room.

On September 25 the house became The Haven as our Nana and Papa moved in!

Soccer Season

CHOOSE A MOTIF TO MATCH YOUR THEME

(TOP LEFT) Soccer is a big part of the Anderson's family life in summer, and the octagon quilt pattern is the perfect design for capturing the flavor of the sport. This two-page spread uses 16 photographs cropped with an octagon template (Creative Memories) and one $3^1/_2$ x $4^1/_4$" for the center of a page. Assemble octagons as shown, add "stitching," stickers (Creative Memories), and journaling, and fill in spaces as desired with triangles cut from $1^3/_4$" squares.

Kerrie S. Anderson, Clovis, California

Beehive

BUILD YOUR OWN HONEYCOMB

(LOWER FAR LEFT) "Our first summer as beekeepers was filled with excitement. My husband and oldest son were mentored in the skill by a good friend. The rest of us spent a lovely afternoon caring for the hives and snapping photos." Mary found $2^5/_8$" hexagons, which she cut from a homemade stencil, to be the perfect symbol for this theme page. She used two plain-paper hexagons for journaling and yellow ovals for bees.

Mary Lindberg, Hessel, Michigan

Nana and Papa's New Home

SCRAPBOOK A WORK IN PROGRESS

(LOWER LEFT) Roberta's family was so excited that her grandparents were moving to town that they visited the construction site of the new home almost daily. The boys were comfortable in the place before moving day—after all, they'd spent many happy days playing there already! Roberta cut her photos using an octagon stencil (Creative Memories), journaled in the white spaces, and added border pieces cut from brown packing paper. The border pieces are made from one edge of the octagon shape.

Roberta Mealey, Midland, Michigan

Four Generations

WHEN MY MOTHER DIED in 1994, my sisters and I found among her things a box of quilt blocks. I washed and pressed the blocks, then photocopied them, reducing the size so they'd fit in my album. I made a page with the blocks, including a photograph of my twin sister and me, mother, grandmother, and great-grandmother. I believe it was my great-grandmother who made the quilt blocks, which are wonderful examples of fabric from the 1930s and 40s.

I love color, and fabrics used for quilt-making come in wonderful colors and patterns, including batik. Recently introduced to "foundation pieced" quilting, I've experimented with a few patterns and some of my favorite fabrics. Making color copies of the blocks allows me to keep a record of my experiments in my photo album. Then I can give the "real" blocks away in a finished project and still have a copy for myself. This, in turn, gave me the idea to color copy fabrics onto acid-free, photo-safe paper and design pages in my albums with my own custom-made papers.

—*Faye Weber, Boise, Idaho*

Christmas Eve

ACCENT WITH CHRISTMAS PLAIDS

The Smiths attend a children's mass at church each Christmas Eve. When they get home, they pose for pictures before going to bed. Using these printed (Hot Off the Press) and plain papers leaves no doubt about what special time this page commemorates. The octagons measure 3⅜" across, squares measure 1⅜", and the triangles are 1" squares cut in half diagonally. Use a banner stencil (Provo Craft) for the title.

Jeannie Smith, Baden, Pennsylvania

Me and My Penguins

PIECE TOGETHER A PASSION FOR PENGUINS

Penguins are everywhere! Kathleen added a different touch to this octagon template (Creative Memories) page by cropping two photos into elongated shapes. In addition to shapes cut in polka dot papers (large dot by Paper Patch, small dot by Hot Off the Press), the page is accented with letter stickers (Creative Memories), a penguin paper (Hot Off the Press) border, and even a penguin die cut (Handmade Scraps, Inc.).

Kathleen Groeschen, Mason, Ohio

Opening Doors

ADD AN EXTRA LAYER OF JOURNALING AND PHOTOS

Pages with doors and windows that open to reveal stories and more photos are easy to make and hold fun surprises. This page has opening flaps on five of the hexagons.

Inspired by Patricia Brazil, Martinez, California and RaeAnn Struikmans, Temecula, California

Our Wedding Day

1. *Assemble your honeycomb page as desired using photographs and printed papers (Keeping Memories Alive). The hexagons for this page were made using a template (Puzzlemates), and they are adhered to a plain cream-colored background. Once the page is together, decide which hexagons you want to open and carefully cut around five sides with a craft knife, using a ruler as a guide. The side left intact becomes the "hinge."* *(Figure 1.)*
2. *Once you've cut the doors, mount a photograph or plain paper for journaling to the back of the page, behind each of the cutout hexagons. (Figure 2.)*
3. *Add journaling as desired. (Figure 3.)*

Four Generations of Beauty

Using templates can cut your planning time in half—no need to measure and figure! And the Puzzlemates system (Paper Adventures) will ensure precision shaping for your quilt pieces. One template will allow you to make four different size designs—this one is the extra large. The corners are decorated with triangles made from 2½" squares.

Alison Bergquist for Puzzlemates, Brea, California

Our First Home Together

FRAME YOUR PHOTOS IN BLUE AND WHITE

Here is another way to create the hexagon effect. Carolyn used 1" strips of printed papers (Creative Memories) to frame her photographs. Cut the strips of gingham and star paper into 2³/₄" segments, then cut a 45° angle in one end. Arrange the strips around the photographs as shown, and "bind" the quilt with a plain blue border.

Carolyn Perfetti, Franklin, Ohio

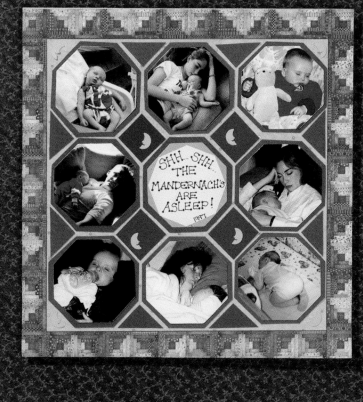

Our Honeymoon

MAKE A HONEYCOMB OF MEMORIES

As used here, the hexagon stencil (Creative Memories) shows off distant beach scenes as well as floral close-ups. To completely fill the page, use partial hexagons at the top, bottom, and sides of the page. Carolyn left space at the bottom for journaling.

Carolyn Perfetti, Franklin, Ohio

The Sleeping Mandernachs

ADD A QUILTED BORDER

Who would think that sleeping people can make such a fine scrapbook page? This hexagon (Accu-Cut clear die cut for cropping photos) quilt page is accented with moon punches (Marvy Uchida) and is set on a paper with a Debbie Mumm printed log cabin border (Creative Imaginations).

Cindy Mandernach, Grand Blanc, Michigan

Emily

SHOW YOUR CHILD'S MANY FACES

What better way to use many similar pictures than in a quilt? Jennifer made the paper pieced bunny by copying the design from Emily's outfit. The shapes and letters are made with nested templates (Provo Craft), and the background uses printed paper (Keeping Memories Alive).

Jennifer Borowski, Princeton, New Jersey

Sweet Dreams

MAKE A SLEEPING BABY QUILT

What says "quilt" more than a sleeping baby? A paper crimper (Fiskars) and lace stickers (Mrs. Grossman's) are used to create a ruffle and lace edge around this octagon quilt. The title is done with an outline of alphabet stickers (Creative Memories) over patchwork printed paper (Frances Meyer). Rub On Stars (Provo Craft) create the background, and photos are cropped with an octagon template (Creative Memories) and arranged on a striped paper background (NRN Designs). The bear is from a puzzle template (Provo Craft), and its features are added with circle and oval punches.

Rita Brei, Mission Viejo, California

Diamonds, Triangles, and Other Geometric Shapes

Some speculate that the geometric quilts produced in England echo the beauty and precision of patterns enjoyed by the Romans at the height of the Roman Empire. The Romans used combinations of triangles, squares, and rectangles—shapes familiar to any modern quilter—in their tiled walls and floors. Patterns such as Flying Geese, Variable Star, and the Tumbling Blocks (shown here) do, indeed, mimic these mosaic tile designs. The simple shapes make them perfect for scrapbooks.

Yellow Tumbling Blocks Probably made between 1940 and 1950, this quilt was purchased by Eugenia Mitchell, founder of the Rocky Mountain Quilt Museum, from St. John's Episcopal Church in Denver. From the collection of the Rocky Mountain Quilt Museum. 1991.1.95.

Tumbling Blocks

COMBINING DIAMONDS of light, medium, and dark papers in certain ways creates wonderful optical illusions—is it a block? Is it a star? Here, it's both. In the original design, the "stars" are actually five small diamonds. Pam substituted larger stars in order to incorporate photos.

Pam Frye, Denver, Colorado

Supplies needed
Diamond and star pattern (page 125), 1 medium toned solid paper, 4 light printed papers, 2 medium toned printed papers, and 4 dark printed papers.

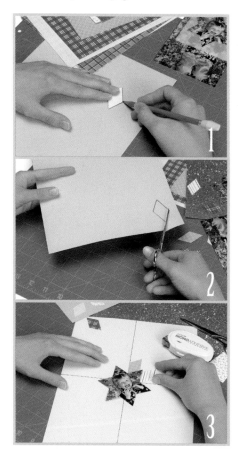

1. *Using the pattern provided on page 125, make a diamond template. Trace the outline on your paper. (Figure 1.)*
2. *Cut the diamonds. (Figure 2.) For this page you'll need 20 solid yellow, 5 yellow checkered, 15 red plaid, 4 pale orange plaid, 8 striped, 4 beige plaid, 3 green splatter, 2 green and white plaid, 2 blue and white print, and 1 green and red plaid diamonds. (See page 127 for paper sources.)*
3. *Using the star pattern provided on page 125, make a clear template. Position it over the desired part of the photograph, trace, and crop.*
4. *Find the center of your background (we used oak tag paper). Position a star photograph in the center and begin building blocks around the photo as shown, leaving the background to show through as parts of blocks and for journaling. (Figure 3.)*
5. *Fill the page to the edges using partial diamonds and ³/₈" strips of plain yellow paper.*
6. *Journal in the open stars.*

To make a 12 x 12" page *The page shown here is 8¹/₂ x 11". For a page of any other size, proceed as described above until you reach the edges of your page, then fill in with partial shapes as needed. See pages 12 and 13 for more ideas on resizing.*

Springtime Tumbling Blocks

STACK LOTS OF PHOTOS ON YOUR PAGE

Kathryn couldn't bear to part with any photographs of her girls, so she used the classic tumbling block quilt idea to incorporate ten of them on one page. One diamond template (see page 122) and five printed papers: green splotch (Provo Craft), pink plaid (MPR Associates, Inc.), green plaid and pink dot (The Paper Patch), and floral (Frances Meyer) make the blocks. Arrange the diamonds as shown around your photos. Kathryn let several of her photos "step out" of the blocks. A ¹/₄" border binds it all together.

Kathryn Neff, Bel Air, Maryland

Barnes Family Quilt

TUMBLE ACROSS TWO PAGES

For a two-page spread, form one continuous pattern by splitting the center blocks straight down the middle. Elizabeth used five printed papers: green plaid and peach polka dots (Hot Off the Press), blue gingham, checks (Provo Craft), and floral (Paper Patch). She cut the paper with a diamond shaped stencil (Creative Memories) and cropped the photos with a hexagon stencil (Creative Memories). The title is done with letter stickers (Provo Craft).

Elizabeth Barnes, Federal Way, Washington

Red and White Delight

LAYER BOLD COLORED TRIANGLES

One size of triangle and paper strips do it all for this complex-looking but so-easy-to-make page. Cut red triangles by halving ¾" squares. Arrange them around two 3⅝" and two 2¼" photos mounted on ivory as shown, framing two of the photos and the outside edge of the page with ¼"-wide strips. Journal on the borders and add decorative "stitching" to the pieces.

Donna Pittard, Kingwood, Texas

Thanksgiving Quilt

ADD A FLYING GEESE BORDER

The Flying Geese pattern in autumn colors is perfect for Thanksgiving. The triangles are cut from 1½" squares using five printed papers: four plaids and a check (The Paper Patch). The background for the triangles is a green bird track paper (MPR Associates, Inc.), which is bordered with rust paper, and the page background is cream. Use fancy scissors to cut mats for the photos and punch leaves of various sizes. Adhere to page as shown.

Beverly Love, Paducah, Kentucky

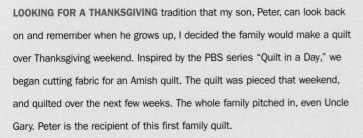

Lester Don Thatcher
My oldest brother
His wife Marsha (Black)
Darren & Brenda & Robin Renea.
Jeff & Ann.
Reed & Sakurako.
Josh, Joy, & Julie

Sibling Symmetry

MAKE A SHOWCASE FOR TINY PHOTOS

Joy wanted to be able to view pictures collected over the years of her many brothers and sisters. The quilt idea is perfect because her mother loved to quilt. Joy used two printed papers (Karen Foster Design) to make triangles from $1\frac{1}{4}$ x $\frac{7}{8}$" rectangles. Arrange triangles as shown, pieced together with photos cropped to 1 x $1\frac{1}{4}$" rectangles, and use as page border.

Joy Candrian, Sandy, Utah

Quilt in a Month

LOOKING FOR A THANKSGIVING tradition that my son, Peter, can look back on and remember when he grows up, I decided the family would make a quilt over Thanksgiving weekend. Inspired by the PBS series "Quilt in a Day," we began cutting fabric for an Amish quilt. The quilt was pieced that weekend, and quilted over the next few weeks. The whole family pitched in, even Uncle Gary. Peter is the recipient of this first family quilt.

This page documents the making of our "Quilt in a Month." I added a few Roman Stripes to my page, but kept decorative elements to a minimum in order to journal the story behind the quilt.

—Diane Eppestine, St. Louis, Missouri

BLOCK PATTERNS *such as many of those featured in this book were the most popular in early America. The individual blocks are small and easy to work with. And with the Puritan work ethic being what it was, that meant you could travel with your work, leaving no time for idle hands. Block patterns often reflected everyday life with tree, flower, and animal motifs.*

Pocket Page

MAKE A BASKET TO HOLD GOODIES. Pocket pages are great for holding memorabilia that you might want to remove from your book to look at from time to time. And what better than a basket for holding your treasures? Theresa used a traditional basket quilt motif, which is comprised of light and dark triangles.

Theresa Lindamood, Sacramento, California

1. *Begin by cutting five 2" squares of light patterned paper (MiniGraphics) and four 2" squares of dark floral paper (Keeping Memories Alive). Cut the squares diagonally in half to make 10 light and 8 dark triangles. (Figure 1.)*
   • Make pocket in the background paper by slashing it horizontally in half, leaving 1" on right and left edges uncut. Once the paper is cut, mount it onto another backing paper, being sure not to glue over the opening.
2. *Place your photos in the bottom corners as shown. Arrange the triangles in basket design as shown on a separate piece of paper cut to an 8 x 8 x 11¼" triangle and adhere to page being careful to leave pocket opening unobstructed. (Figure 2.)*
3. *Cut a 7½" half-circle handle that is ¾" wide from your dark paper and adhere it to the back of the top edge of the basket. (Figure 3.)*
4. *Journal a title on a stencil banner (Provo Craft).*

Michael is an Angel

CREATE A QUILT WITH PUNCHES

Square and building block punches (Family Treasures) are used to create the pastel tumbling blocks with Michael's angel face. Rita used a lace stencil (Conners Collectibles) to emboss a heavenly border, and embossed accents of bows, hearts and bows (Conners Collectibles), pinwheels (Family Treasures), and a frame (Conners Collectibles). The large bow is a die cut (Accu-Cut), and the letters are punched from extra photos with Alphabet Punches (Family Treasures).

Rita Brei, Mission Viejo, California

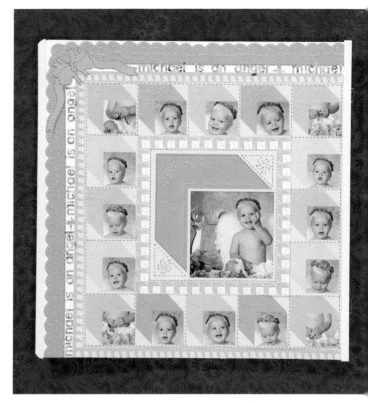

Tulip Quilt

LET THE PICTURE TELL THE STORY

"When I tried to scrapbook this picture, I was really stuck. It was just a random photograph with no cute story behind it. When I noticed one of my mother's many quilts in the background, my problem was solved!" Annalia made tulips to match those in the quilt. The patterned papers, pomegranate spatter dot (Provo Craft), pink gingham (Frances Meyer), and green plaid and scribbles (Colors by Design) are complemented with plain red, mint, and forest green paper. A template appears on page 124.

Annalia Romero, Summerville, South Carolina

Niagara-on-the-Lake

MAKE A BLACK AND WHITE PINWHEEL

Caroline "borrowed" this idea from
another layout she saw in a back issue
of *Memory Makers* magazine (issue #2,
Winter 1997). Make a triangle template
by cutting a 4" square in half diagonally
and use this for cutting mats (Caroline
alternated black and white paper). Trim
photos to be slightly smaller than mats.
Add a border of colored paper strips
cut with deckle scissors, and punch
snowflakes from extra black and
white photos.

Caroline LeBel, Toronto, Ontario

Through the Leaves of Time

MAKE A FIVE-GENERATION
FAMILY TREE

When Lorraine's first granddaughter was
born in 1988, there were five generations
on both her and her husband's sides of
the family. Getting everyone together for
a group photograph wasn't possible, so
she solved the problem by making a quilt
page with individual photos. Splatter
background and printed leaf papers
(Keeping Memories Alive) are used with
plain green card stock. The leaves (see
template on page 126) are finished with
black pen "stitching."

Lorraine Stevens, Lynnwood, Washington

Ocean Waves

USE PHOTOS AS QUILT "FABRIC"

Elsie has lots of photos and lots of quilt patterns, and she decided to combine the two for this page.
Triangles cut from 1½" squares of matching landscapes dramatically showcase the central photo.
Mount triangles on black background as shown and add title and stitching
with a silver pen and wave ruler (Creative Memories).
Ocean Waves is the name of the quilt pattern and also is
appropriate to the subject of the photographs.

Elsie Duncan, Unity, Saskatchewan

Quilt with a Shape Cutter

Creating quilt motifs is a snap with the help of a shape cutter. For this page, Dawn used Lighthouse Memories' triangle cutter. While the shapes are a bit rounder than those on most triangles, the nine shapes on this page are absolutely identical!

Dawn Mabe, Broomfield, Colorado

1. *Place the photograph to be cropped on a cutting mat. Decide which part of the photo will be the center of your shape, and position the template over that area. Use the template to determine the size of your cropped photo. (Figure 1.)*
2. *Adjust the shape cutter to your chosen size and place it over the photograph in the position determined by the template in Step 1. Press down lightly and rotate cutter arm to cut photograph. (Figure 2.)*
3. *To assemble the page shown here, place nine cropped photos as shown on a printed paper (Provo Craft) background. Embellish page with ⅝" paper strips and border stickers (Provo Craft) and add journaling as desired. (Figure 3.)*

The shape cutter also makes matting your photographs a breeze. Simply extend the arm of the cutter to desired size for your mat and cut a paper shape. The mat will be exactly the shape of your photo, just slightly larger!

Christmas at Beesons

PIECE TOGETHER THEME PHOTOS

Linda decided to take a photograph of her family members holding their Christmas stockings. A 45° diamond quilt template provided just the right shape. The page is embellished with Christmas stickers (Printworks) and letter and number stickers (Provo Craft) and then "stitched" with a white pen.

Linda Beeson, Ventura, California

Geese in Flight

QUILT A POKÉMON™ BIRTHDAY

The theme of the party, and the page, is Pokémon. The Geese in Flight pattern uses sets of triangles from 1" squares with a darker on the bottom and lighter on the top of each set. And it works great with these primary colors! Linda used photographs, printed papers, wrapping paper, and a birthday card to piece together this page of 172 triangles and 4 squares. Oh, add another 39 triangles for the border! The central character is freehand drawn, and the border has "stitched" journaling.

Linda Strauss, Provo, Utah

Family Heritage Album

Rosario's sole inheritance from her father is a collection of vintage family photographs. She sorted the photos and created several albums. The albums are either 5 x 7" or 8 x 10", which Rosario feels are the most comfortable sizes to look at as bedtime stories. The quilt theme has been encouraged by her experiences as a teacher and as a patron of her local scrapbook store, Catch a Falling Star, in Minnesota.

The page at right is titled "Peace Time (1947) Family Portrait Quilt." The Crazy Quilt of Mother

Finding comfort in a smile

1975

Oxford Ohio

December 31, 1917 – Ibajay, Capiz, Philippines

To Miss Raymunda Guerrero, Normal Hall, Manila –
A token of sincere affection to my dear Manang and to remind her of Oping.
Journaling at the back of this picture: from photo album of Auntie Mundang.

and Son at left was adapted from a quilting book on stars of the states. The before and after pages below show the photograph that kept Rosario inspired while she was studying in the United States and separated from her children and a photograph of the reunited family. And the Wreath of Hearts commemorates the rediscovery of a reason to smile.

Rosario's vintage photographs are black and white or sepia toned, and she chose soft and understated colors with which to show them off to best advantage. She has carefully documented the history of each photograph on the back of the page. The photograph on the page below left is from 1917 and is a tribute to Miss Raymunda Guerrero from Normal Hall, Manila.

Rosario L. Guerrero, Bear Lake, Minnesota

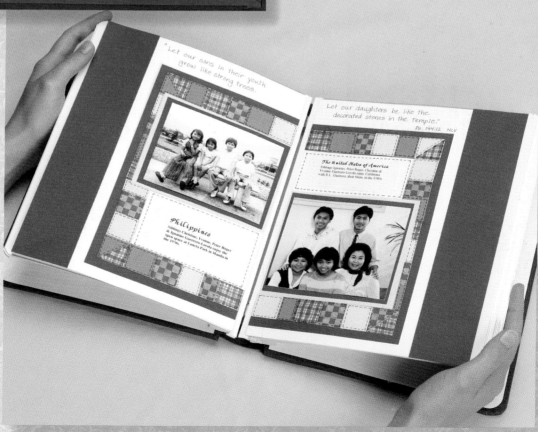

Miss Hannah 1999

Circles, Hearts, and Flowers

While many of these quilt patterns are a little more difficult to make than those from simple squares and diamonds, they were very popular all across America. Quilts with hearts, flowers, and wedding rings told of love and marriage. And the Dresdan Plate, shown here, makes a wonderful frame for your favorite portraits. With the number of possible color choices, it's hard to imagine a photograph that wouldn't work with this design.

Dresdan Plate This pattern was popular during the 1930s and 1940s. The quilt was made by Bess Appel and donated to the museum by Ella Appel of Boulder, Colorado. From the collection of the Rocky Mountain Quilt Museum. 1996.2.4

The Dresdan Plate

A TEMPLATE FOR A DRESDAN PLATE QUILT is made by drawing a circle to fit your page, drawing a smaller circle within that to the size you want your center, then dividing this circle into 16 or 20 equal parts. Marilyn used the 16-piece technique here and cut each section from a different printed paper. She made the center hole large enough to accommodate this sweet photo of Hannah.

Marilyn Garner, San Diego, California

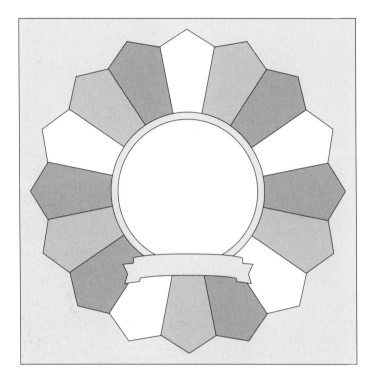

Supplies needed

Pattern (page 122), 4 pastel printed papers, 4 light printed papers, and 4 medium printed papers.

1. *Using the pattern provided on page 122, make a template for the segments. Trace the shape onto printed paper. (Figure 1.)*
2. *Cut the shapes. For this design, you'll need shapes of 16 different papers. (Figure 2. See page 127 for paper sources.)*
3. *Find the center of your page and draw a 1" circle in the center. Place the segments around the center, making sure they are properly aligned, and adhere to page. (Figure 3.)*
4. *Crop a photo to desired circle size (5½" shown here) for center, mat, and adhere.*
5. *Add a title to a banner (ChartPak) and mount below photo.*

To make an 8½ x 11" page *Reduce the template on a copy machine to 70%. Proceed as above and center the plate on your page. Add borders if desired. See pages 12 and 13 for more ideas on resizing.*

Dresdan Plate

PAINT A PASTEL PORTRAIT

Darlene scanned an old photograph and repaired it using photo software. She then printed it in black and white and colored it with acid-free pencils. The restored photograph looks wonderful as the center of a Dresdan Plate motif (see template on page 123) made with coordinating pastel printed papers (The Paper Patch). "Stitching" is added with opaque gel pens and shaded with colored pencil.

Darlene Bruehl, Dayton, Tennessee

Veronica's Page

CREATE DRESDAN FANS

Janet divided a traditional Dresdan Plate (see template on page 122) into four parts and used them to create a fan-like motif in the corner blocks. Because the photos were taken against a busy background, Janet decided to silhouette-cut them, leaving the natural shadow intact. She used printed paper (Provo Craft) for the fan and center motifs. A silver pen was used for the hand-drawn "stitching." These photographs were taken by Veronica's father just 24 hours before she left this world, a victim of heart disease.

Janet Oegema, Bowmanville, Ontario

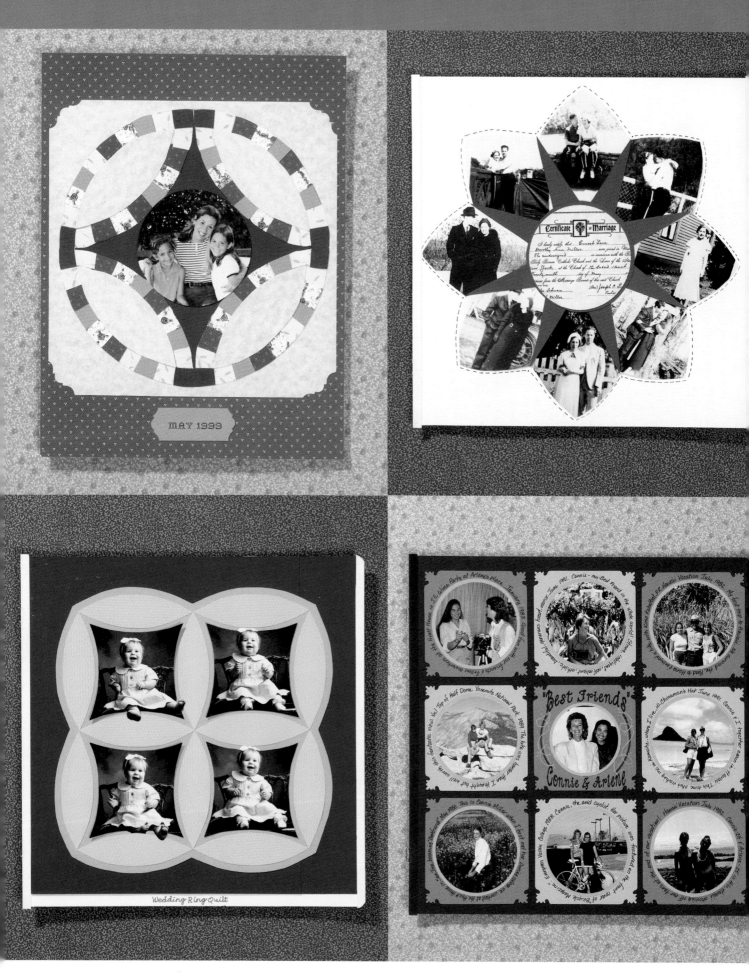

MAY 1999

Wedding Ring Quilt

"Best Friends"
Connie & Arlene

Double Wedding Ring
COMPLEMENT A TINTED PHOTO

(FAR UPPER LEFT) During a visit to her stepdaughter's home, Shari was introduced to scrapbooking and photo tinting. She used her newly acquired skills to create this Double Wedding Ring page. Each piece is cut individually (see template on page 124) from various papers (Keeping Memories Alive, Frances Meyer)—somewhat time-consuming but the results are worth the effort! A date is added using the font Home Sweet Home (Microsoft Publisher). The page is set on a printed paper (Close to My Heart) background.

Shari Dinnen, Mount Dora, Florida

The Good Old Days
MAKE A MOTHER'S DAY MEMORY PAGE

(UPPER LEFT) Nancy's parents are in their 80s. Their photograph book was disintegrating, so Nancy decided to make a new album as a Mother's Day gift. She copied the original photos and assembled them using the Shadow Star motif she found in a quilt book (see template on page 124). Nancy used her parents' marriage certificate in the center, and the page separates their dating years from their married years in the album.

Nancy Thomas, Avon Park, Florida

Wedding Ring
CROP OUTSIDE THE LINES

(FAR LOWER LEFT) Using textured paper that matches her daughter's dress, Rita created this Wedding Ring quilt page using four charming photographs. Notice how different bits of each photograph silhouette outside the lines of the template. This page is easy to make using a Stens-a-Quilt template (Classic Trio).

Rita Brei, Mission Viejo, California

Best Friends Quilt Page
MAKE CIRCLES IN THE SQUARES

(LOWER LEFT) Arlene made this quilt page for her best friend, Connie. The photos are cropped into 2³/₄" circles and matted with circles of plain paper ¹/₈" larger than the photos. Mount the circles onto 3½" squares with punched corners using an edge punch (McGill). You'll get the added surprise of another design where four corners come together. This really stands out on the black background. Add journaling around the circles.

Arlene Santos, Milalani, Hawaii

Made Especially for Me
by Grandmother

MY GRANDMOTHER, who lived to be 103 years old, made this Sunbonnet Sue quilt for me when I was a little girl. While in New York, I found this same motif on a rubber stamp, and used it to create a page in her honor. I began with a photograph of my quilt in the center, then added photographs of Grandma Moll at various stages of her life.

—Judy Weston, Poplar Bluff, Missouri

Sewing

DAWN USED A REAL QUILT TECHNIQUE FOR THIS PAGE—SEWING.
She decided to substitute real stitching for glue when assembling this page. The paper will eventually dull your machine needle, but you can easily make a few pages before replacing the needle.

Dawn Mabe, Broomfield, Colorado

1. *Using a heart template (Family Treasures), draw a heart in the center of a 3¼" square piece of cream cardstock. Using a craft knife and a cutting mat, cut the heart from the cardstock, saving the negative image. (Figure 1.)*

2. *Place 5 heart frames over 3⅛" square photos, and 3 frames over 3⅛" squares of printed fabric. (Figure 2.)*

3. *Using a sewing machine, sew around the squares about ³⁄₁₆" in from the edges. (Figure 3.)*

4. *Mount the sewn squares onto 3½" squares of blue cardstock.*

5. *Sew one plain cream square with journaling to a blue square.*

6. *Arrange the squares as shown and adhere to page with printed paper (Keeping Memories Alive) background.*

We (Heart) Our Mother

STITCH A PATCHWORK OF HEARTS

Julie made this page for her mother's birthday. She used photographs of her mother, her sister, and herself. To achieve a "country" look, she cut the hearts and buttons irregularly by hand. Each heart and most buttons have two layers, and stitching is added with both black and white pens. She actually framed this one for her mother and made a laminated color copy for herself.

Julie Walkup, Silver Spring, Maryland

Heart of Our Hearts

MAKE A BRIDAL WREATH PAGE

The name of this quilt block, Bridal Wreath, doesn't actually connect with two-year-old Megan, but it's an easy block to piece with paper, and the large hand-drawn hearts are good showcases for photos. The light green plaid (Sonburn) and other printed papers (The Paper Patch) are cut into four 1½" triangles for the center, four 3" triangles for the corners, and hand-drawn 1½"-wide wreath sections for connecting the hearts, then mounted on the checkered background. Use letter stickers (Frances Meyer) for title.

Glenna Murdock, Loveland, Colorado

SENTIMENT WAS DEEPLY

rooted in the quilts that grew under the fingers of young girls dreaming of the days when they would be wives and mothers in their own homes. Hearts were often incorporated in the designs for central motifs, and border patterns were carefully plotted so that there would be no broken ends nor twisted lines of stitching. To the superstitious, broken ends were an omen of trouble to come.

—*From* The Standard Book of Quilt Making *by Marguerite Ickis*

Quilted Hearts

PIECE TOGETHER A SCRAP QUILT

Jan was inspired to make a quilt page when she saw all the pretty papers at her local scrapbook store. Using sixteen different papers (Hot Off the Press, Colors by Design, The Paper Patch, MiniGraphics, Northern Spy, Karen Foster Design, Provo Craft, and E.K. Success) creates the look of a true scrapbag quilt. Crop photos with handmade heart template, and use a medium heart punch (Marvy Uchida) for the motifs in alternating blocks.

Jan Petro, Summit Hill, Pennsylvania

Wedding Rings

IT'S EASIER THAN IT LOOKS!

Caroline used a Stens-a-Quilt template (Classic Trio) to create this elaborate-looking but surprisingly easy-to-make page. She used two coordinating printed papers (Hot Off the Press) and similar plain paper for titles. Punched silver snowflakes are placed where the quilt points meet.

Caroline LeBel, Toronto, Ontario

Our Ringbearer

PUNCH AN ELABORATE DRESDAN ROSE

Erin loves color, texture, and shapes and always wanted to quilt—unfortunately, she's not a very good seamstress. But with the variety of punches and papers available, Erin can put her creativity to work making patterned papers for her scrapbook. Here she used a circle cutter for the three center circles (3⅞", 4⅜" and 4⅞") and a variety of punches: ¼" circle, maple leaf, small heart, daisy, small daisy, and sun. Five plain papers combine with doilies (Pebbles in My Pocket) that are highlighted with a gold gel pen to create the Dresdan Rose motif (see template on page 125). A title is added on a stencil banner (Provo Craft).

Erin Crawford, San Leandro, California

Matt's
School
Days...

Start
to
Finish

From his first day
of kindergarten in
1982 until his high
school graduation
in 1995, Matthew
was an exception-
al student and
an outstanding
musician. We are
so proud of the
fine young man
he has become.

Patchwork Potpourri

There are perhaps as many quilt designs as there are fabrics—
or for us, papers—to choose from. This chapter presents a collection of miscellaneous pieced designs, all appropriate for
your scrapbook.

This design, Old Red Schoolhouse, was traditionally just
that—made of red fabric on a contrasting solid ground. But
don't limit yourself. Your house can be any color.

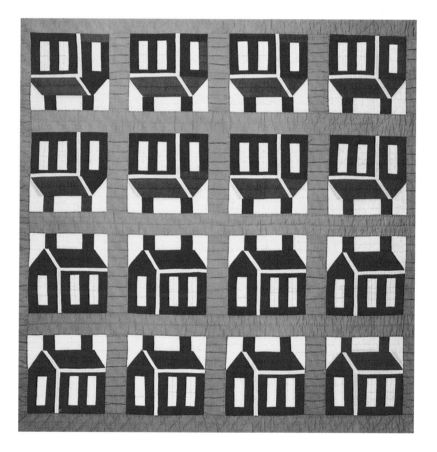

Old Red Schoolhouse Made by Margaret Fay Garrity (1868 – 1956) who was
born in Middletown, New York, and moved to Denver with her family in 1881.
After the death of her husband, Margaret made her home with relatives, living with each for three or four months at a time. As repayment for hospitali-
ty, she made and offered quilts. In 1926, this was given to a niece, Ruth
Jennings Hanson, who passed it on to her daughter, Marjorie Hanson
Sweeney, who donated it to the museum in 1991. From the collection
of the Rocky Mountain Quilt Museum. 1991.1.10.

Old Red Schoolhouse

THIS IS A QUICK AND EASY QUILT PATTERN that lends itself well to photographs, and the theme makes it a natural showcase for these school photos of Matt. The only tricky part to putting together this page was remembering junior high school geometry! A clear plastic T-square is helpful for making accurate rectangles.

Debra Fee, Broomfield, Colorado

Supplies needed
Patterns (page 126), solid white, solid red, and solid green paper.

1. *Make templates using patterns provided on page 126 and trace shapes for roof pieces onto red paper. (Figure 1.)*
2. *Cut roof pieces. (Figure 2.) For house and chimneys, cut one rectangle 3⅝" x 4¼", one rectangle 4 x 4¼", and two rectangles 1¼" x 1⅓". For the border, cut four 2" wide strips of green paper.*
3. *Glue down the 2" border to a white background, then assemble schoolhouse within resulting 8" square. (Figure 3.) Add stitching, photographs, and journaling.*

To make an 8½ x 11" page *Omit the borders on the sides, make the top and bottom borders 1¾" wide, and center the schoolhouse on the page. See pages 12 and 13 for more ideas on resizing.*

Merry Christmas 1998

ADAPT A TRADITIONAL QUILT BLOCK

Glenna found a pattern for the Pine Tree Block in a quilt book. She eliminated the four background pieces that make the motif into a square block and used just the actual tree pieces. To make the trees, draw a triangle with a 6¼" base and 7" sides. Mark the center point of each side and the center point of the base. Connect the center marks to create templates for diamonds and triangles. Turn the pine trees into Christmas trees by topping them with stars. Glenna used a variety of printed papers (Keeping Memories Alive), star stickers (Frances Meyer), and a white pen to add "stitching" and journaling.

Glenna Murdock, Loveland, Colorado

Tartan Twins

USE FABRIC SCRAPS IN YOUR BOOK

Kathy sews clothing for all her grandchildren (and their dolls!), and decided to incorporate scraps of the fabrics in her quilted scrapbook page. Each block is 4" square and the blocks are separated with ¼" strips of black paper. The fabric triangles are cut from 1¼" squares, the paper triangles are cut from 1" and ½" squares; the basket triangle is half of a 2¼" square. To keep the fabric from raveling, she pressed it onto a heat-set backing before cutting out the shapes. If you're concerned about fabric deterioration, you could create a similar effect by color copying the fabrics onto acid-free paper.

Kathy Vaden, Brunswick, Maine

Use Nested Templates

Callahan
1999

Intricate precision cutting of various sizes is a snap with nested templates (Provo Craft). This neat little template lets you quickly and accurately cut squares with rounded corners in nine graduated sizes. Jennifer used letter stickers (Provo Craft) for her title and added accents with punched leaves. The background is a printed paper (Provo Craft).

Jennifer Blackham, West Jordan, Utah

Susan Carol Candrian Jeppesen
Mike's only sister & the youngest in the family.
Garry, Candria, Erin, Brant, Kirk, & Michael

Family Trees

CREATE A PINE TREE BORDER

This page is simple yet effective. Joy cut a 6$\frac{1}{2}$ x 7" piece of green printed paper (Karen Foster Design) and arranged photos of various sizes on it. She then framed that with $^3/_8$" strips of red printed paper (Karen Foster Design), accented in the corners with heart and button stickers (Creative Imaginations). Triangles cut from $^7/_8$ x 1$^3/_8$" rectangles and $^3/_8$" squares of the green paper are combined in a pine tree pattern and used to border the bottom of the page. Title and journal are done with Dimples font (Karen Foster Design).

Joy Candrian, Sandy, Utah

Love Makes the Family

CREATE A HERITAGE QUILT

Showing her children photos of their ancestors is important to Kimberly, and a quilt page seemed a good way to incorporate several photos. She looked through her quilt magazines for patterns that she could adapt to use with paper. A variety of printed papers—green squiggle and large watercolor roses (Keeping Memories Alive) and green stitched roses (DJ Inkers)—add to the quilted look. All the designs here begin with a 1" square and are combined to make 3" blocks that are bordered with ½" strips. From there you either cut the square diagonally or horizontally to create designs with smaller pieces.

Kimberly Wise, Goodlettsville, Tennessee

Thanksgiving 1998

MAKE A QUICK AND EASY QUILT PAGE

This special page celebrates the first Thanksgiving the Hubers were able to spend together as a family. The scenes actually look more like Christmas, and that's because it was a perfect day for taking the Christmas family photo. Melissa freehand "stitched" hearts and stars and creatively accented them with little patches of paper.

Melissa Huber, Lynchburg, Ohio

THROUGHOUT HISTORY, *inspiration for quilt designs has come from sources as varied as presidential campaigns and vegetables. But perhaps the most appealing motifs result from a stroll through the garden. Flowers, vines, ladybugs, butterflies, and leaves all make attractive patterns for fabric quilts and scrapbook pages alike.*

Paper Folding

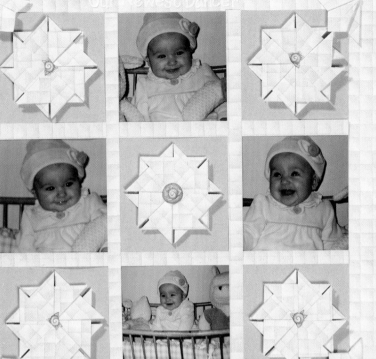

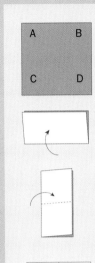

USE PAPER FOLDING for a dynamic page. Simple yet elaborate-looking paper folding will add new dimensions to your scrapbook pages. Cheryl used the triangle fold and added kite folds in the corners. For each large motif you'll need eight 2" squares of Debbie Mumm printed paper (Creative Imaginations) folded with the triangle fold. The corners take one 2" square each, folded with the kite fold.

Cheryl Lindsay, Oceanside, California

ASSEMBLY

Holding two pieces with closed points facing same direction, slide single flap of one triangle between two flaps of the other triangle. Snug them up tightly so that the bottom points meet. Secure with adhesive on back of single flap of inserted piece. Repeat with remaining triangles, sliding first triangle into last to finish.

Triangle Fold

1. *With pattern side facing up, fold C and D to A and B and crease.*

2. *Open flat, fold A and C to B and D and crease.*

3. *Open flat and turn paper over with pattern side down.*

4. *Bring A to D, forming a triangle, and crease.*

5. *Open flat, fold C to B, forming a triangle, and crease.*

6. *Holding folded corners in either hand, push fingers toward center as shown. Move the flap in your left hand toward the back and bring flap in your right hand forward, forming a layered triangle.*

Kite Fold

Follow steps 1 to 6 of Triangle Fold.

7. *Bring top right flap perpendicular to center fold.*

8. *Use a pencil to open the edges of raised flap.*

9. *Keeping center creases aligned, remove pencil and press flat, creasing both sides of the new "kite" shape.*

10. *Turn piece over.*

11. *Repeat Step 7.*

12. *Repeat Step 8.*

13. *Repeat Step 9.*

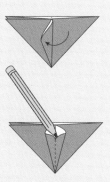

PAPER FOLDING technique by Kris Mason of Folded Memories and Laura Lees of L Paper Designs. For more paper folding ideas, see *Memory Makers® Memory Folding™.* (Ordering information is on page 127.)

Planes and Bows

USE FUN AND TRADITIONAL MOTIFS

Traditional quilt motifs (see templates on page 122) are great for scrapbook pages, and these are perfect for baby photos. Donna used lavender (Hot Off the Press) and yellow (Keeping Memories Alive) printed papers for the airplanes, pink with polka dots (Print Works) for the bows, and mounted both on powder blue paper (Keeping Memories Alive). She punched yellow stars for the corners of both pages to further tie them together.

Donna Pittard, Kingwood, Texas

Halloween 1998

MAKE A PUMPKIN PATCH(WORK)

The Goulds love Halloween, and Jennifer made this nine-patch quilt to commemorate the family affair. Cut four 4" squares from each of the two printed papers (The Paper Patch). Cut these squares in half diagonally to make triangles and arrange as shown. Mat photos on plain paper (the squares are 4⅝"), add "stitching" as desired, and mount on the page, overlapping as shown. Pumpkin stickers (RA Lang) and heart patches complete the page.

Jennifer Gould, Costa Mesa, California

Home Grown

QUILT IN AUTUMN TONES

Susan loves collecting paper as much as collecting fabric—and she has lots of both. But she admits that quilting with paper is far easier! This page uses 2" squares and a crazy quilt-type of arrangement of geometric shapes cut from various printed papers (The Paper Patch). To make the orange paper shapes in the center, cut a 4" square diagonally in quarters. A double matted rectangular photo takes the center focus, and the page is accented with matted computer font lettering and a pumpkin die cut (My Mind's Eye). The "Home Grown" title font (Inspire Graphics) features seasonal art.

Susan Combs, New Albany, Indiana

The Wonder of Christmas

MAKE A SUNBEAM BLOCK

Amy has made so many quilted scrapbook pages that she's published a whole book of them called *Piece by Piece Quilted Memory Pages* (All American Scrapbook Company). This page features the easy-to-make Sunbeam pattern. It uses only two shapes—one for the photos and the other for plaid and gingham papers (The Paper Patch)—and is embellished with jounaling and pen stitching.

Amy J. Shepherd, Butler, Pennsylvania

A Quilting Bee

EVERY TUESDAY, a group of wonderful women gather at the local firehouse and work on their quilts. While I don't quilt myself, I love the company of this group, so I join them and work on my scrapbook pages. This page honors their talent and friendship. I had several photocopies made of the page, and at least two of the group have framed copies and hung them on the wall of their quilting space.

Nancy Sennett, Keene Valley, New York

A Sampler Album

Marilyn has made so many quilt pages in so many styles for her scrapbooks that she's lost count. The sampling shown here is a wonderful example of how versatile quilt motifs can be. They can be used to convey any theme imaginable, depict any season, and represent any holiday. Marilyn uses die cuts, punches, pre-made templates, templates she hand-makes from patterns in quilt books, stickers, pen stitching and more—whatever it takes to get the desired results.

The Autumn Sampler page uses a variety of printed and plain papers that are punched or cut, along with die cut reindeer and freehand borders. Back to School is embellished with stickers, punched and die cut apples, leaves, and stars, and lots of pen stitching. The Green Leaves Appliqué is a fine example of how the positioning of one leaf can be very effective.

Girls' Night Out is an adaptation of the very traditional Wreath of Roses quilt design. Marilyn added a nice touch with birds holding the title banner. The Easter Sampler page uses a combination of eight printed and seven plain complementary papers pieced together with thin strip borders and accented with pen stitching.

Marilyn Garner, San Diego, California

Crazy Quilts

The Crazy Quilt is an indigenous American quilt style. Briefly popular during the late 1800s, it is being revived today along with many other forms of folk art. Random shapes are joined with fancy stitching to create a block. Cloth quilts are typically made with brocades, velvets, and silks. For paper quilts you can get the same effect with velvet, suede, or velour paper, metallics, even embossed, crimped, or tightly pleated paper and, of course, photographs. When making a fabric quilt, it's easiest to cut shapes with straight, not curved, edges. But with paper, anything goes!

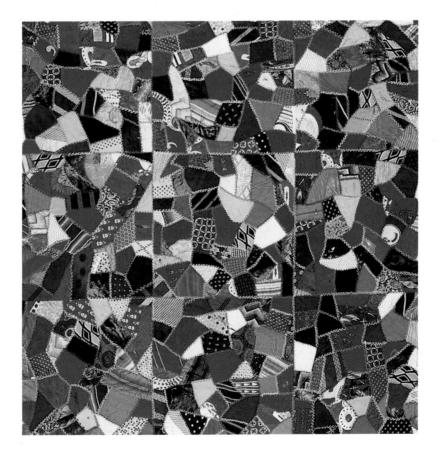

Crazy Quilt Made by Eugenia Mitchell in 1979, this quilt contains a mix of tie fabrics and dress velvets, sateens, and rayons. From the collection of the Rocky Mountain Quilt Museum. 1991.1.25.

Crazy Quilt

A CRAZY QUILT PAGE can have any number of pieces in any shape, just as long as the pieces fit together like a puzzle to fill your page. For this page, Joy chose a variety of fabric-like papers, including suede, and assembled the quilt on cardstock, leaving a ½" border all around.

Joy Carey, Visalia, California

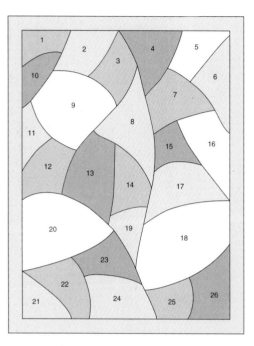

Supplies needed

1 sheet each of 10 medium toned printed papers, 2 medium to dark suede or velvet papers, 4 medium toned solid papers and 3 light printed papers, and cardstock for the background.

1. *Cut a piece of plain white paper to the size of your scrapbook page minus ¹/₂" all around. Draw a puzzle of random shapes and number each section. Make a photocopy of your pattern, and cut out the individual pieces. Trace each pattern piece onto a different paper or photograph. (Figure 1.)*

2. *Carefully cut the shapes out with scissors. (Figure 2.) You may use the same paper more than once, but don't put two of the same papers next to each other. Jot down the pattern piece number on the back of the paper or photo. This will make reassembly easier.*

3. *Mark a ¹/₂" border around your cardstock background. Using your original pattern as a guide, piece the quilt together and adhere it to the cardstock. (Figure 3.)*

4. *Outline each piece with a black marker. This will help distinguish the pieces and make the spaces appear more even.*

5. *Add stitching and journaling with metallic and gel pens.*

To make a 12 x 12" page *The beauty of the crazy quilt is that you can easily make it any size you want. Simply continue drawing a pattern to fill your page. See pages 12 and 13 for more ideas on resizing.*

A Crazy Quilt

MAKE A SHAPE FOR EVERY PHOTO

Sandria's Crazy Quilt page represents her family growing larger and larger. She started in the middle with a rectangle and drew her design out from there. She created the whole design in different colored paper, then cropped photos to fit. It was challenging and fun to find just the right photograph for each quilt piece. Sandria left a couple of pieces plain for journaling and title, and "stitched" it all together with black pen.

Sandria Holva, Bangor, Pennsylvania

Crazy Baby

PUT "LEFTOVER" PHOTOS TO GOOD USE

Quilts are a visual reminder of family love and togetherness, and you can use quilt layouts to express the same ideas in your scrapbook. Angie made this Crazy Quilt page with various photos of her son. It took some time to crop and arrange the photos and paper, but the end results are worth the trouble. The pen stitching adds to the effect and the page is embellished with stickers (Mrs. Grossman's).

Angie Sipe, Waverly, Iowa

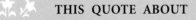

THIS QUOTE ABOUT *Crazy Quilts comes from 1897 pattern instructions: "Crazy patchwork has now become so popular as to require but little instruction. As the name indicates, it is simply sewing together odd pieces of silk, satin, plush, etc., in a way so that the angles may somewhat imitate the craze or crackle of old china, from which all this kind of work derives its name. The ornamenting of the seams with fancy stitches in bright-colored silks gives a very pleasing effect. Of course, no directions can be given as to the colors to be used, as this is where the taste of the worker is displayed." From* Crazy Quilts *by Penny McMorris. New York: E.P. Dutton, Inc., 1984.*

Pieces of My Heart

PUT MISCELLANEOUS
PRINTED PAPER TO WORK

Have you ever bought papers just because they look great, and then get home and have no idea what to do with them? That's how this quilt page came to be. Eileen freehand cut printed papers (Frances Meyer) and photographs, mounted them on a plain background, and added stitching, journaling, and tiny hearts with a black pen.

Eileen Iaquinto, Higley, Arizona

Crazy Cats

EVERYONE IN MY FAMILY is crazy about cats. When my sister Barb Jensen made this quilt as a wedding gift for our sister Kathy and her husband, Craig, we were all drooling! I have a box overflowing with odd scraps of paper and they were perfect for creating the "kitty blocks" from the quilt as a background for this page, which is "quilted" entirely from scraps. I added a title with letter stickers (Provo Craft).

—Mary Lavery, Quincy, Illinois

Build a Crazy House

Betty loves Crazy Quilts, and for her scrapbook she took the idea a step further and created a Crazy House. All the doors and windows open, and she carried her theme even further by having them open to photographs of a friend's fabric quilts. The various printed papers (Keeping Memories Alive) are cut into random shapes and "stitched" together with black pen. The chimney "smoke" and door and window handles are done with stickers (Mrs. Grossman's).

Betty Folmar, Spokane, Washington

Stamping Patterns

WITH A RUBBER STAMP AND INKPAD, you can create custom-made papers for quilted scrapbook pages. There are hundreds of different types of stamps to choose from. Select those that will support your theme.

This page was created in the Crazy Quilt tradition. Sarah used printed papers from Susan Branch Designs (Colorbök), and stamped using the technique described below. She chose plaid papers, which provide a grid for evenly spacing stamped motifs. She used a rose stamp (Guadalupe's Rubber Stamps) and a daisy stamp (Stamp Francisco) to enhance the printed papers, and letter stamps (All Night Media) for titles.

Sarah Fishburn, Fort Collins, Colorado

Crazy For You

1. *Tap the rubber side of the stamp on the inkpad. (Figure 1.) Be sure the stamp is evenly covered with ink. If your stamp is larger than the pad, or if you want to use more than one color, ink the stamp with colored markers.*

2. *Apply the stamp to the paper before the ink dries. (Figure 2.) Press down firmly. Do not rock or wiggle the stamp, or you may blur the image.*

3. *Assemble your Crazy Quilt with random shapes as desired.*

Monarch Magic
USE PHOTOS OF EVERY SIZE

Barbara spent a special weekend, a thank-you gift from a friend, with her husband in Pacific Grove, California, visiting the nature habitat and observing monarch butterflies over-winter. Because they were allowed only on designated paths, she ended up with a few close-up shots and many distance shots. The Crazy Quilt design let her use both to best advantage. She used fancy scissors (Fiskars), border punches (McGill), and butterfly and lace papers (Lasercraft and Hallmark) to decorate the quilt page.

Barbara Christmann, Rohnert Park, California

QUILT SYMBOLISM

Crazy Quilts typically use fabrics with different textures and sheens. In addition, many incorporate hand-embroidered "pictures" of children, dogs, birds, and flowers. There is a symbolism for many flowers used in these quilts.

> *Rose / Love*
>
> *Daisy / Innocence*
>
> *Pansy / Remembrance*
>
> *Willow Branch / Mourning*

Crazy Quilt
PATCH TOGETHER YOUR FAVORITE HOBBIES

Juanita decided to do a Crazy Quilt page with each patch featuring a creation from one of her hobbies. Included here are sewing, flower arranging, crocheting, embroidery, and ceramics. She freehand drew a ruffled border, added journaling and "stitching," and accented the page with theme stickers (Mrs. Grossman's).

Juanita Owens, Arvada, Colorado

Appliqué

In the Midwest, perhaps because fabric was scarce, even small pieces and bits of goods were precious. The pieced quilts from this region are known for their tiny, carefully cut pieces. When materials became more readily available, covers of the appliquéd type rose to favor in that region. This type of quilting has become the most important contribution made to the craft by American quilters of the late seventeenth and early eighteenth centuries. And they are much easier to do with paper—just cut and paste!

Four Seasons Made by Ruth Mosher and Nancy Offutt of Colorado Springs as a donation to the museum, this appliqué quilt contains some three-dimensional work. From the collection of the Rocky Mountain Quilt Museum. 1997.4.1.

Spring 2000

APPLIQUÉ IS ONE OF THE MOST VERSATILE quilt techniques you can use in your scrapbook. You can find lots of patterns for flowers, leaves, birds, and other shapes in quilt books, or you can draw your own, as Marilyn did for this page. She decided to make her page copying the Spring block of the Four Seasons Quilt.

Marilyn Garner, San Diego, California

Supplies needed

1 light printed paper, 2 medium printed papers, 1 dark printed paper, 1 medium solid paper, and 3 dark solid papers.

1. *Freehand draw or copy flowers and leaves in various sizes, and one bird. Make templates for the shapes as described on page 9. Trace the shapes onto your chosen paper. (Figure 1. See page 127 for papers used here.)*

2. *Carefully cut the shapes out with scissors. (Figure 2.) This page has three large and seven small flowers, three large and six small leaves, and one bird.*

3. *Freehand cut a circular branch of brown paper. Using the diagram as a guide, place and adhere the branch, a central photograph, flowers, leaves, and bird on the page. (Figure 3.) For a dimensional effect, tuck some of the flower petals under the photograph as shown.*

4. *Using a small flower punch, punch two yellow centers for each flower and adhere.*

5. *Pen stitch flowers and add journaling or title.*

To make an 8¹/₂ x 11" page *Begin with a branch that is shaped like a tall "C" and arrange photo and other pieces to fit around it. See pages 12 and 13 for more ideas on resizing.*

Christmas Poinsettia
APPLIQUÉ WITH PUNCHES

JoAnne is an avid quilter, and she uses her quilt books for inspiration for scrapbook pages. This type of quilt, laborously made in fabric, was easily made in paper using common punches. The poinsettias are each made with five medium hearts and the berries and leaves are punched with holly border punch (All Night Media) and teardrops and large holly (Family Treasures). JoAnne freehand drew the large scallops to get just the right size for her page, and she used a circle cutter for the center photo and mat.

JoAnne McPherson, Martinez, Georgia

Greetings from Our House to Your House
APPLIQUÉ A WREATH OF ROSES

Linda made this quilt page from an idea in a quilting magazine using a variety of printed papers: green and white and scribble (Keeping Memories Alive), and others (The Paper Patch). This design was one panel of the quilt, and the actual measurements of the block were 12 x 12". She altered it slightly by using punches for a few of the pieces (leaf, egg, and tulip), but for most she used the patterns provided in the magazine. See page 124 for templates.

Linda Beeson, Ventura, California

THE PATTERNS FOR *appliqué quilts from the Midwest were developed largely from the common flowers and natural objects of the region. Such are the Rose of Sharon, Tulip, Sunburst, Birds on the Wing, and many others. The proudest boast a woman of those days could make was to be able to say she had originated a quilt pattern of her own.*

—*From* The Standard Book of Quilt Making and Collecting *by Marguerite Ickis.*

Stenciling

STENCILING IS AN INTERESTING WAY TO CREATE the effect of appliqué without cutting out lots of little pieces of paper. It uses a painting technique called "dry" application—you use such a small amount of paint that it won't rub off when touched. Cynthia chose velour paper (Wintech International) as her background. The effect is wonderfully soft, warm, and fuzzy—perfect for showing off a baby portrait. This page was made with Crisp 'n Clean Stencils (Provo Craft) and Dauber Duos (Hero Arts).

Cynthia Castelluccio, Carrollton, Virginia

1. *Place the stencil over the velour paper and secure it to the paper with masking tape or repositionable adhesive. It's important that the stencil stay firmly in place. Gently daub the paint over the stencil, changing colors as desired. Centering the stenciled area, cut the paper into a 4⅛" square. Repeat until you have four stenciled squares.*

2. *Using a coordinating color of sewing thread, decoratively stitch around the shape—this highlights the stencil and makes it look as if the shapes are sewn to the blocks.*

3. *Cut mats and plain blocks as follows: six 3¾" squares and two 4½" squares of medium blue cardstock, four 3⅜" squares of lavender cardstock, and four 3⅛" squares of velour. Crop your photo as desired (this one is 6¼ x 4½") and mat it with three or four colors of paper or cardstock and trace around the mats with a silver pen.*

4. *To assemble page, arrange the medium blue blocks with the smaller ones in the corners. Add the lavender cardstock and blue velour blocks to the corners and the stenciled blocks to the middle blocks as shown. Trace around the blocks with a silver pen. Mount matted photograph in center of page as shown. For the final touch, make 16 little bows of satin ribbon and adhere to page.*

The Economy Jr. Women's Club Quilt

MAKE A QUILT FOR CHARITY

Each year, the Economy Jr. Women's Club makes a quilt and raffles it off. The proceeds go to award scholarships to graduating seniors and to various community charities. Jeannie made this page to commemorate one such auction, using fabric from the raffled quilt on her page. Templates are provided on page 124.

Jeannie Smith, Baden, Pennsylvania

Six Generations

APPLIQUÉ A HERITAGE PAGE

Nicole made this heritage page for her daughter. She collected photographs from her great aunt, the only of the oldest generation living at the time—in Holland! Nicole used a stencil (Stampendous!) for her design. The stencil is 4 x 4", so she drew it on a piece of paper, scanned it into her computer, and enlarged it to fit her 12 x 12" page, and cut and pieced her "quilt."

Nicole Ramsaroop, Orlando, Florida

Sunbonnet Sue

USE PHOTOS AS "FABRIC"

(FAR UPPER LEFT) The Sunbonnet Sue quilt pattern was very popular during the 1930s and 40s. You can find variations on the pattern in many traditional quilt books. We've provided the pattern used here on page 125. Elsie cut the pieces out of photos of some of her favorite flowers. She used a stencil for the lettering (Plaid) and corner motifs and a silhouette punch (Family Treasures) for the accent tulips.

Elsie Duncan, Unity, Saskatchewan

The Neffs

APPLIQUÉ A TITLE PAGE

(UPPER LEFT) Kathryn wanted a title page for her family album, and decided on a quilt theme. She went to the library and checked out several quilt books for ideas. She used punches, including tulip, diamond, and square, and added borders of paper strips.

Kathryn Neff, Bel Air, Maryland

While Dad's Away...

QUILT A ROSE OF SHARON

(FAR LOWER LEFT) Karen's two loves are quilting and scrapbooking. She's currently working on a queen-sized appliquéd Baltimore Album/ Rose of Sharon Quilt and she borrowed a design for this page. (Karen says scrapbooking is a lot faster than quilting!) This page uses two sizes of heart templates (Family Treasures) and three sizes of circles (two punches and one small template). Grid the background in with pencil, then "stitch" with pen and erase the marks.

Karen Weiss, Edmond, Oklahoma

Tyler and Marci

APPLIQUÉ A BALTIMORE ALBUM PAGE

(LOWER LEFT) Nancy is working on a Baltimore Album quilt, and this page reflects one of the blocks she's completed. She found the pattern in *Baltimore Beauties and Beyond* by Elly Sienkiewicz (C&T Publishing). Using printed papers (Hot Off the Press), she copied the leaves and hydrangea to frame a photo of her cousin and her son. A leaf template is provided on page 124. The lettering is freehand.

Nancy Schroeder, York, Maine

Emily's Heirloom

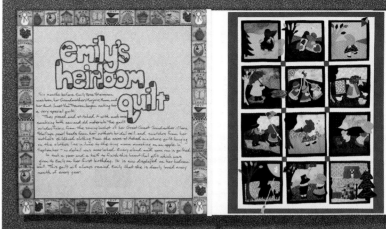

SIX MONTHS BEFORE Emily Rose Stevenson was born, her grandmother, Marjorie Mann, and her aunt, Janet Van Treuren, began making her a very special quilt.

They pieced and stitched it with much care, combining both new and old materials. The quilt includes fabric from the sewing basket of her great great grandmother, Clara Stallings, pearl beads from her mother's bridal veil, and swatches from her mother's childhood clothing. From the cross-stitched miniature quilt hanging on the clothesline in June to the tiny work munching on an apple in September, no detail was overlooked. Every cloud and corn row is quilted.

It took a year and a half to finish this beautiful gift, which was given to Emily on her first birthday. It is now displayed on her bedroom wall. This quilt will always remind Emily that she is dearly loved every month of every year.

I knew I wanted to include it in Emily's scrapbook, but I wasn't happy with pictures of the quilt—they didn't show enough detail. I decided to take twelve pictures—one of each block—and "piece" them together with paper pieces. The blocks are much clearer, and the facing border page tells the story.

—*Tammy Stevenson, Florissant, Missouri*

Appliqué Album

Annette loves appliqué quilts and has found wonderful ways of re-creating them with paper. She uses punch art, die cuts, stencils, templates, and any other way of making shapes you can imagine, including freehand drawing, to create these colorful and imaginative pages.

The very creative and complex-looking Wedding Shower title page is made up of only four shapes—leaf, flower, heart, and circle—with an umbrella in the center. The tulips on the page at lower left are made with squares and triangles, the hearts are punched, and the large flowers are a combination of punches and shapes cut from templates. The nine-patch quilt at lower right of this page also uses a variety of paper-cutting techniques, and all three of these pages are accented with the use of fancy scissors to trim the blocks.

The Patchwork Christmas page at left has a traditional border of triangles, and Annette pieced together the hearts in the same way a Crazy Quilt is made. Summer 1997 has brightly colored blocks arranged in a variation of a traditional Fruit Basket motif. Annette's dramatic use of primary colors is very effective for a summer page.

Annette Gymonpré, Tallahassee, Florida

The Bear Family

1897

Trapunto

Trapunto quilts are among the most elegant. They were in vogue in America during the late eighteenth and early nineteenth centuries, and they often consisted of only one fabric with lots of stitching. These quilts have a raised design, creating three dimensions. They were backed with a loosely woven fabric, and the quilter would separate the threads and force bits of cotton or wool through the holes until the front motif was padded.

The scrapbooker has several options for creating this stitched look: Embossing will give you the raised effect, while paper piercing and pen stitching can be used to effectively create a tone-on-tone look.

Lazy Daisy Variation Made by Lura Lee Lemon and Jean Lemon Benson, sisters who lived near Boulder, Colorado, this quilt was probably crafted during the second quarter of the nineteenth century. It is exquisitely hand pieced, quilted, and stuffed. Donated to the museum by Judith Trager. From the collection of the Rocky Mountain Quilt Museum. 1997.7.3.

Lazy Daisy Variation

THE BEAR FAMILY 1897 PAGE, like the quilt it's fashioned after, uses a combination of patchwork and trapunto stitching. The star and chevron patches are made with diamonds cut from red and blue cardstock and the feather-stitching pattern (StenSource International) is traced using a light box. The background is cream-colored cardstock.

Joy Carey, Visalia, California

Supplies needed

Diamond pattern (page 124), feather-stitching pattern (StenSource International), red, blue, and white paper.

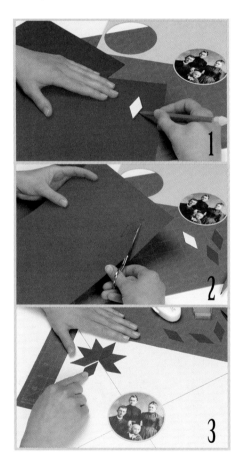

1. *Using the template on page 124, trace 24 red and 24 blue diamonds. (Figure 1.)*
2. *Carefully cut the diamonds out. (Figure 2.) Be as accurate as you can here or the stars will not go together well. Because it is nearly impossible to cut perfect diamonds, you may trim them to fit when you assemble them.*
3. *To find the center of your page, lightly mark from corner to corner diagonally across the page. Place matted 3½" round photo in center. Beginning in the corners, assemble stars, then add chevrons as shown. (Figure 3.)*
4. *To create the trapunto effect around the photo, use a light box and pen stitching to trace the feather pattern onto the page with a light tan pen. Use the same pen to "stitch" a crosshatch pattern in the squares created in the pieced border.*
5. *Add shadowing with tan chalk and a cotton swab.*
6. *Pen stitch around the edges of the red and blue diamond shapes. Add title or journaling.*

To make an 8½ x 11" page *To re-create this pattern, eliminate the center two chevrons top and bottom, and feature an oval photograph. See pages 12 and 13 for more ideas on resizing.*

Here Comes the Bride

PIERCE A PORTRAIT FRAME

It all started for Judy when she paged through some of her quilting books (which have gathered dust since she started scrapbooking) looking for scrapbook page inspiration. The myriad stitching patterns in these books, such as the feather pattern used here, are perfect for paper piercing. Judy sized the pattern on a photocopy machine. Lay the design on the back side of your paper. Place the paper on a Styrofoam or felt mat, and pierce along the design lines at approximately ⅛" intervals with a push pin or tapered awl. The result is a lovely raised design on the front side.

Judy Nurkkala, Bloomington, Minnesota

Family Ties

STITCH AROUND STICKERS

Florence recently enjoyed seeing a lot of hand-stitched quilts and wanted to try to reproduce that look for a title page for a family album. She decided that using quilter's stencils and a light gray pen worked well. Stickers (Mrs. Grossman's) and a binding of fancy marbled paper (Hot Off the Press) make the design easy to copy. A family name and date could be added.

Florence Davis, Winter Haven, Florida

ONE OUTSTANDING HISTORIC example of a trapunto quilt was called "A Representation of the Fair Ground Near Russellville, Kentucky." In 1931, Eliza Calvert Hall wrote about the quilt in Handicrafter magazine:

"It is the delicacy and accuracy of the figures in this quilt that distinguish it from others of the stuffed variety. It is comparatively easy to quilt a design of large flowers and leaves, but it required more than a needlewoman's talent to outline these horses and other domestic animals that look as natural as life on the surface of the quilt. There are approximately 150 stitches in every square inch of the quilt. Make your own calculation of the total number of stitches."

The answer is 1,200,600.

Embossing

THIS FLOWER QUILT uses a combination of embossing and pen stitching, a very effective way to emulate the look of trapunto quilting. The flower mats were cut using a template (StenSource International), and the page is embellished with punched hearts and a border of pen stitching done using a wavy ruler.

Marilyn Garner, San Diego, California

Embossed Quilt Blocks

1. *Position the embossing template on the front of the paper. Place removable tape along the top and bottom edges of the template to hold it in place. (Figure 1.)*

2. *Turn the paper and template over and place them on a light box. Place more tape along the edges to secure.*

3. *Rub a piece of crumpled wax paper across the area you will be embossing. The small amount of wax makes it easier to emboss.*

4. *Use an embossing stylus like a pencil to trace the inside edges of the template. (Figure 2.) Just outline the shape—you don't have to fill it in. When you're finished, turn the paper over and remove the template.*

5. *Repeat these steps to emboss additional quilt blocks. When you're finished, cut out each block and pen stitch around the designs with black pen. (Figure 3.)*

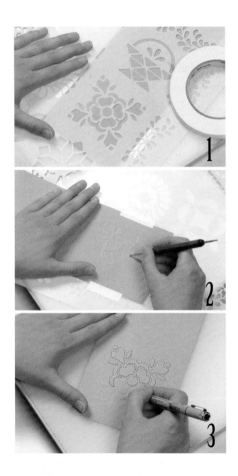

Nikki's Giant T-Shirt Quilt

WHEN MY OLDEST DAUGHTER was ready to leave for college, I presented her with a quilt of all the T-shirts we'd accumulated from trips, fundraisers, and sports events. I thought it would be a fun conversation starter for picnics and football games. The quilt is huge, about 6 x 14 feet. I wasn't really going for a bed size—I just wanted to use all the T-shirts!

When making my scrapbook pages, I didn't want anything that would detract from the pictures of the quilt. I used black and yellow strips to mimic the quilt layout and cut the lettering out of photocopies of the quilt. The worst thing about making the quilt was that I had to put all my scrapbook stuff away because the quilt took up so much space!

—*Susanne Sharp, Port Orchard, Washington*

The Heart of the Matter

EMBOSS A WEDDING PAGE

Darlene stamped and embossed the corners of this page using a stamp (Personal Stamp Exchange). The stitching pattern can be found in many quilting books. Draw the pattern on tracing paper and use an embossing stylus to "stitch" the design. To add dimension, Darlene put chalk on a cotton swab and shaded the quilting lines.

Darlene Bruehl, Dayton, Tennessee

the hunt for the
PERFECT TREE
December 4, 1999

Sampler Quilts

Sampler Quilts were created to show off as many techniques as possible. A Sampler Quilt made by a notable quilt maker to show her favorite or most difficult designs was sometimes referred to as a Legacy Quilt. Sampler pages are great for scrapbookers—you can combine your favorite techniques such as punching, stamping, stenciling, embossing, and stitching—to create a Legacy Page of your own.

Pine Meadows Dorine Tomer of Arvada, Colorado, made this wall quilt in the mid 1990s. The pattern was designed by Jean Wells and was published in the *Quilter's Newsletter Magazine*. Courtesy of Dorine Tomer.

The Perfect Tree

THIS PAGE duplicates as closely as possible the quilt called Pine Meadow shown on previous page, and therefore most of the shapes were hand cut. However, it could go a lot faster using punches. The motifs here have many tiny little cut and pasted pieces, but you could also "fake it" by drawing and coloring. While this page took some time to complete, the results are quite spectacular and very "quilty."

Joy Carey, Visalia, California

Supplies needed

3 dark solid papers, 1 light solid paper, and a variety of plain and printed paper scraps.

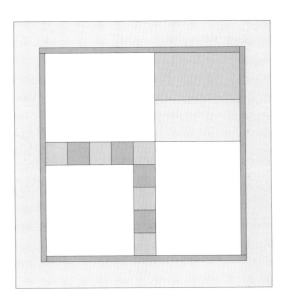

1. *Hand draw and cut 1" appliqué pieces from various printed and plain papers as follows: 10 Ohio Star motifs, 18 pine trees, 1 fir tree, 2 fish, 9 small stars, 1 reindeer and 2 crescent moons. (Figure 1.)*
2. *Following diagram, mark four sections of page. Place photograph in lower left section. (Figure 2.)*
3. *Add border of quilt motifs around photograph. Add remaining photos and appliqué pieces as shown. (Figure 3.)*

To make an 8¹/₂ x 11" page *Mark off a 1" border on all four sides of your page. Divide the center rectangle into four quadrants. Proceed as above, adjusting number and size of appliqué pieces to fit the page. See pages 12 and 13 for more ideas on resizing.*

Steve and RaeAnn

WATERCOLOR A SPECIAL SAMPLER

With one album filled, RaeAnn needed a front page for the second. Following her love for quilts pages, she modified a "Hearts Tied Together" page by Vicky and Diane Higley (Juliet Designs) to include a photograph in the center. After tracing clip art (DJ Inkers) and water coloring the page, RaeAnn tore the edges of the watercolor paper to create a soft edge and then mounted the page on a plain green background.

RaeAnn Struikmans, Temecula, California

Hats Off

CREATE A STICKERS SAMPLER

Her daughter Lauren loves to wear hats, so Karyn took advantage of all those photographs to make a theme page. She used lots of different stickers (decorated hearts Stickapotamus, all others Frances Meyer), various printed papers (Frances Meyer), and a hat die cut (Crafty Cutter). Finally, she accented the page with pen stitching. Title and journaling are done with a letter stencil (Pebbles in My Pocket).

Karyn Noskin, Calabasas, California

Pen Stitch a Quilt

MARY STARTED WITH A SIMPLE page with straight cropped photos of different sizes. But as soon as she got going with her colored pens, the page became a masterpiece! Use any or all of the stitches provided here to make your own sampler page, coordinating the pen colors to match your photos and/or represent a particular holiday. Use a clear plastic ruler as a guide for making the straight stitches, and then fill in with the decorative stitching.

Mary Hammond, Milford, Ohio

To "stitch" a border around your page, place a ruler along the edge where you want the stitching line. For a straight, dashed, or dotted line, use the ruler as a guide and make the markings with your pigment pen. For more decorative stitching, mark your stitching line lightly with pencil. Freehand draw stitches with pen, using the pencil line as a guide.

Dordogne, Août '99

RUBBER STAMP YOUR OWN PRINTED PAPER

Véronique wanted to create a page that features all three of her children and decided that the sampler was the way to go. She hand cut strips and frames of plain and rubber-stamped papers—flower stamp (Magenta), and stripes stamp (Rubber Stampede)—using straight and zigzag scissors. Punched hearts add a loving touch. To complete the quilted look, she drew a sewing needle with a silver pen.

Véronique Grasset, Ruy, France

Keeping Us in Stitches

STITCH TOGETHER PRINTED PAPERS

This quilt idea came to Tammy while she was looking at a collection of silly pictures of her daughter, Emily. She really keeps the family in stitches and she thought, that's it! So she "stitched" the photos and printed papers—patchwork and blue check (Provo Craft), daisy (Frances Meyer), yellow (MPR Associates, Inc.)—together with a white opaque pen.

Tammy Stevenson, Florissant, Missouri

Anne of Green Gables

JOURNAL A PATCHWORK PAGE

(FAR UPPER LEFT) Linda's favorite book is *Anne of Green Gables*. Her trip to Prince Edward Island where the book was written was like a dream come true. Linda chose her favorite passages from the book to journal on the page of photographs from the museum and tourist stops. The antique stickers (The Gifted Line) add a romantic flavor, and the page combines many of Linda's loves: reading, quilting, gardening, traveling, and scrapbooking!

Linda Crosby, Phoenix, Arizona

New Home Sampler

SCRAPBOOK A VISIT FROM RELATIVES

(UPPER LEFT) On Valentine's Day, her mom and other relatives came to Jacksonville to visit Marsha and her family. Most of them came to see the new house. Marsha's daughter Melanie had a new camera and took some of the photos—can you guess which ones? Marsha used lots of coordinating printed papers (MPR Associates, Inc.) to create this sampler page.

Marsha Peacock, Jacksonville, Florida

Zoo

USE POSTCARDS WITH YOUR PHOTOS

(LOWER LEFT) After running out of film at the zoo, Caroline decided to buy postcards that featured her daughter's favorite animals. She then created this sampler page using a combination of the postcards and her own snapshots. And what a great effect! She patched it all together with various brown and green printed papers (Keeping Memories Alive).

Caroline LeBel, Toronto, Ontario

A VERSION OF THE SAMPLER quilt called a Friendship Medley Quilt was often made at a farewell party for a departing neighbor. Each guest brought her favorite scraps and patterns, and each vied with the others to make the best and most unusual block she could, always leaving a place for her signature. The hostess provided set materials, backing, and batting, and the work of quilting was planned and done together. In other cases, the departing neighbor who wanted something to remember her friends by made the Friendship Medley Quilt. She collected enough materials for a block from each of them, made the patchwork herself, and then collected the signatures for each block. In such cases the pattern of all the blocks was usually the same, while the fabrics varied.

The Mennonite Quilt Auction

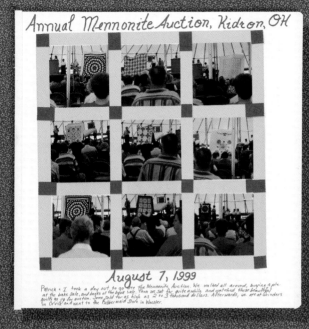

Annual Mennonite Auction, Kidron, OH

August 7, 1999

Patrick & I took a day out to go see the Mennonite Auction. We walked all around, buying a pie at the bake sale, and books at the book sale. Then we sat for quite awhile and watched these beautiful quilts go up for auction. Some sold for as high as 2 to 3 thousand dollars. Afterwards, we ate at Grinders in Orville and went to the Rubbermaid Store in Wooster.

PATRICK AND I TOOK A DAY out to go to the Mennonite Auction. We walked all around, buying a pie at the bake sale and books at the book sale. Then we sat for quite a while and watched these beautiful quilts being auctioned. Some sold for as much as $2,000 to $3,000! Afterwards, we ate at Grinders in Orville and went to the Rubbermaid store in Wooster.

I knew I had to make a quilt page to record the quilt auction. Because it was a bright summer day, I decided to use bright red and yellow for my quilt. I had as much fun making the page as I did watching the quilts at the auction.

—Crista Quinn, North Canton, Ohio

Aa Bb Cc Dd

LOVE

QUILT

This book is like a comforter, a quilt of
    many parts
A keeper of our memories, a place to
    warm our hearts.
The fabric is life's events, those things we
    want to keep
Those keepsakes and photographs placed
    here, not in a heap.
Scraps all stitched together, held fast with
    love and care
Create a family legacy for all to share.
                                    —Author Unknown

ABCDEF
GHIJKL
MNOPQR
STUVW
XYZ

abcdefghij
klmnopqrs
tuvwxyz

FAMILY

Mm Nn Oo Pp Qq Rr Ss

Ee Ff Gg Hh Ii Jj Kk Ll

FRIENDSHIP

Aa Bb Cc Dd Ee Ff
Gg Hh Ii Jj Kk Ll Mm
Nn Oo Pp Qq Rr Ss
Tt Uu Vv Ww
Xx Yy Zz

*Our family's like a patchwork quilt, with kindness
    gently sewn.
Each piece is an original, with beauty of its own.
With threads of warmth and happiness, it's tightly
    stitched together
To last in love throughout the years, our
    family is forever.   —Author Unknown*

PATCHWORK

Tt Uu Vv Ww Xx Yy Zz

Templates

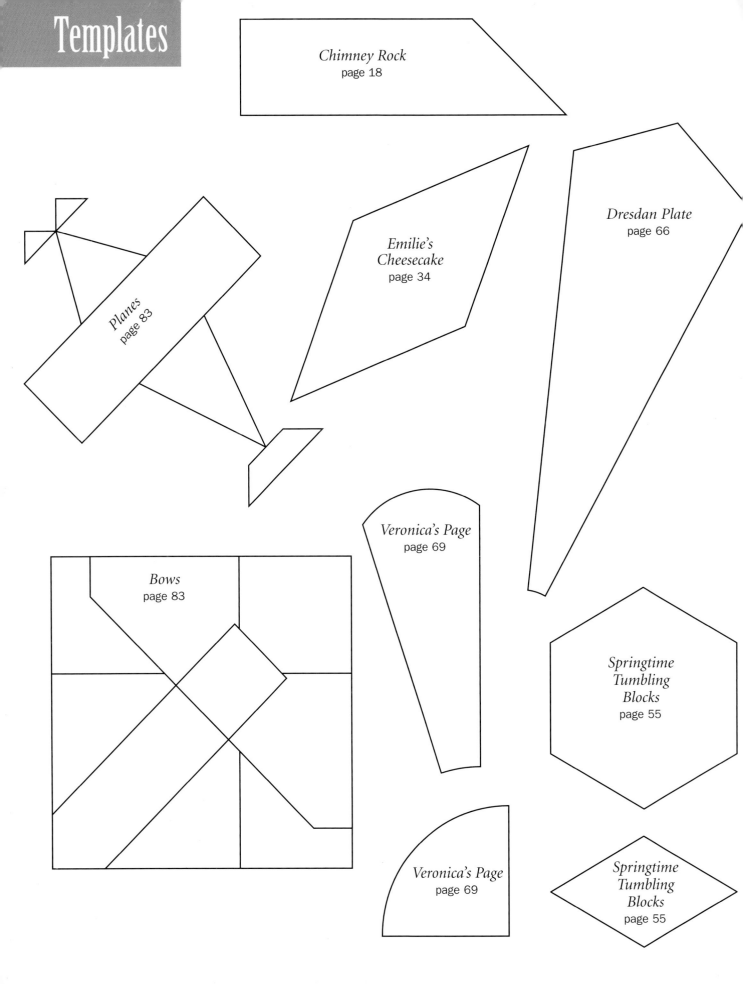

Chimney Rock
page 18

Emilie's Cheesecake
page 34

Dresdan Plate
page 66

Planes
page 83

Veronica's Page
page 69

Bows
page 83

Springtime Tumbling Blocks
page 55

Veronica's Page
page 69

Springtime Tumbling Blocks
page 55

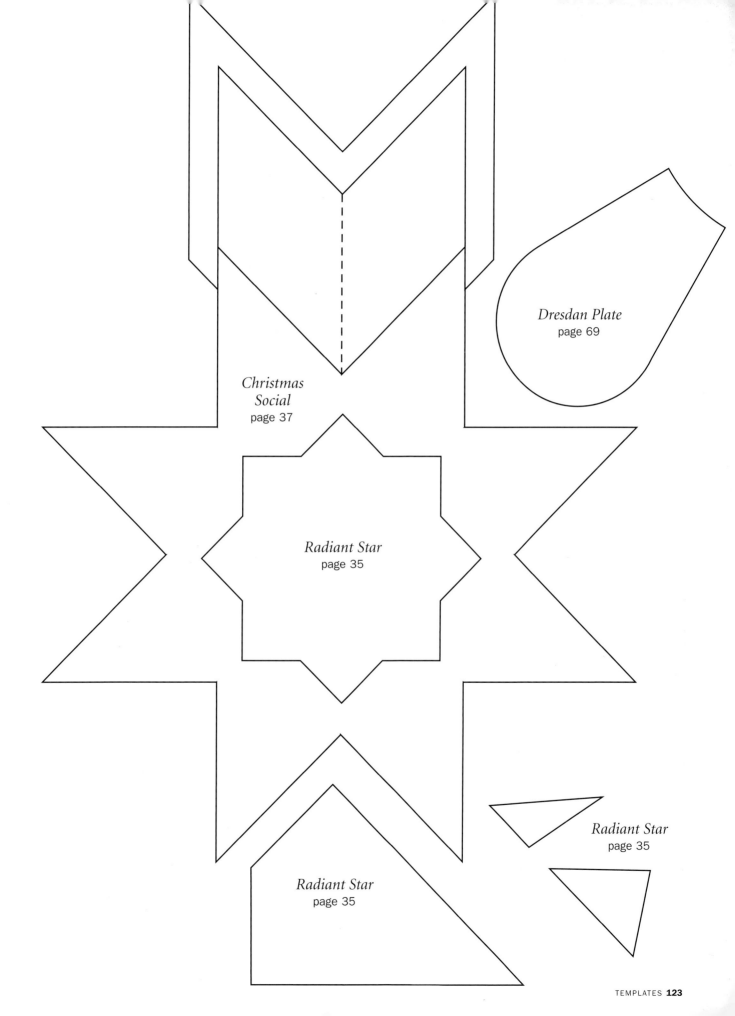

Christmas
Social
page 37

Dresdan Plate
page 69

Radiant Star
page 35

Radiant Star
page 35

Radiant Star
page 35

Templates

The Good
Old Days
page 70

The Economy
Jr. Women's
Club Quilt
page 101

The Good Old Days
page 70

Tulip
page 59

*Greetings from
Our House*
page 99

*Greetings
from Our
House*
page 99

*Greetings from
Our House*
page 99

Double Wedding Ring
page 71

*Tyler and
Marci*
page 102

The Economy
Jr. Women's
Club Quilt
page 101

*Lazy Daisy
Variation*
page 106

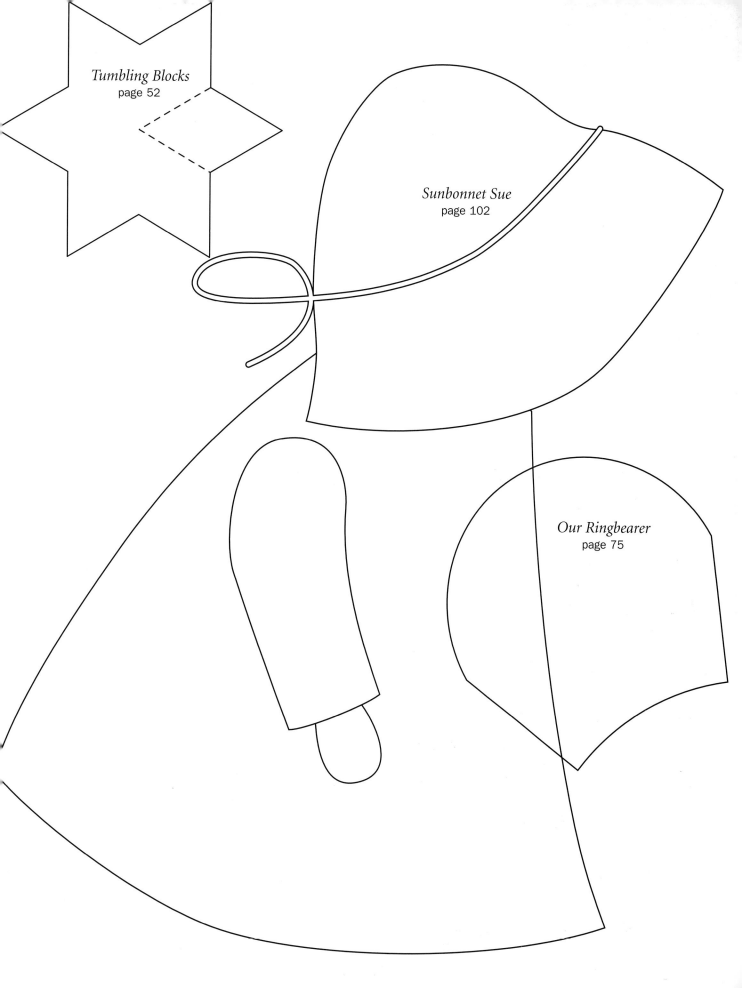

Tumbling Blocks
page 52

Sunbonnet Sue
page 102

Our Ringbearer
page 75

Templates

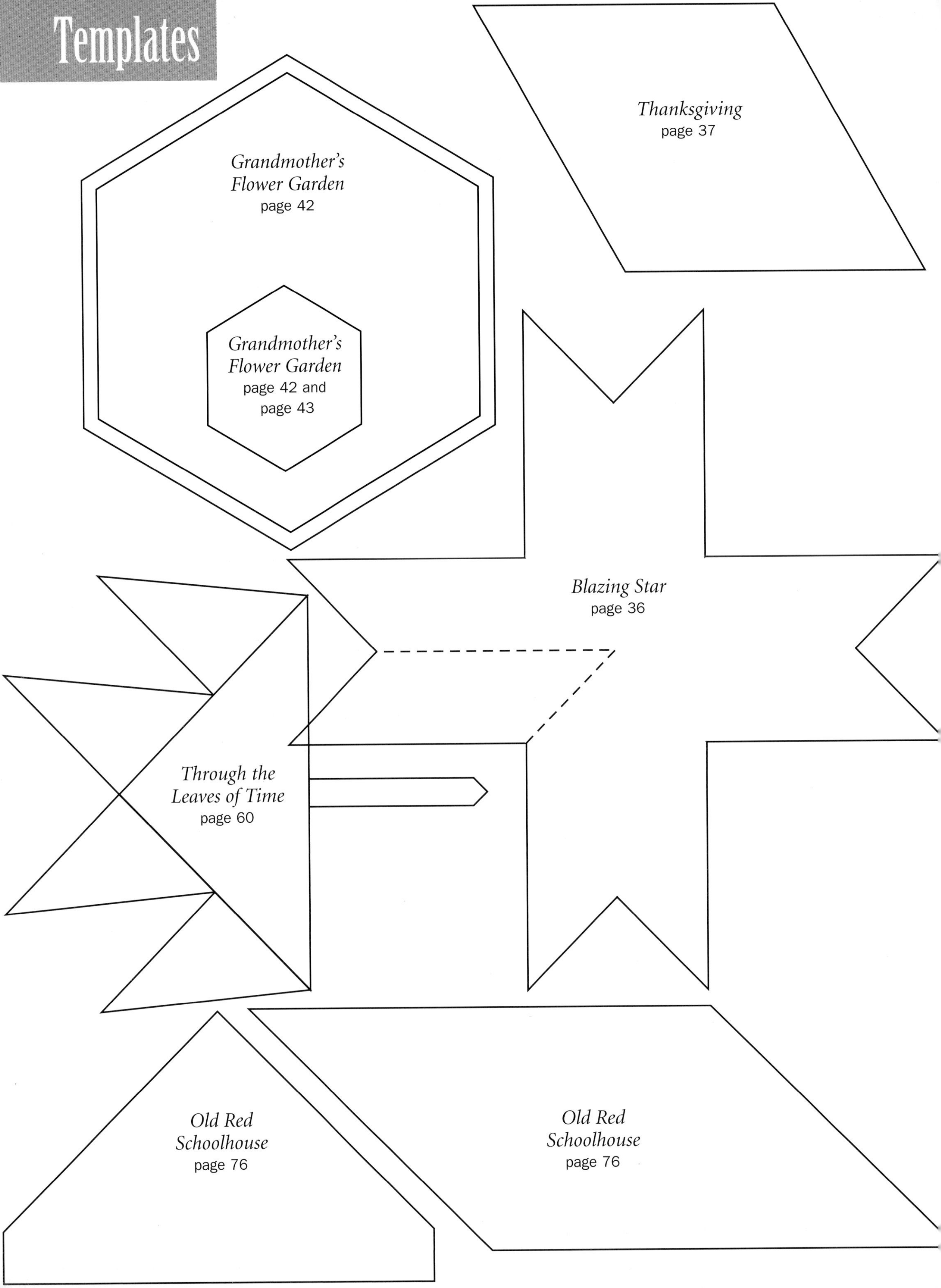

Thanksgiving
page 37

*Grandmother's
Flower Garden*
page 42

*Grandmother's
Flower Garden*
page 42 and
page 43

Blazing Star
page 36

*Through the
Leaves of Time*
page 60

*Old Red
Schoolhouse*
page 76

*Old Red
Schoolhouse*
page 76

Sources and Photo Credits

Page 3
Growing Up
Annette Waisner, Overland Park, Kansas: This design originally appeared in *Memory Makers* magazine issue #2, Winter 1997. Annette used color mounting behind her photos, added a center border, and journaled phrases around the photos.

Page 6
Sources for *You're Five*: floral paper by Current, others by Provo Craft; letters by Provo Craft. Photos courtesy of Lora Mason, Winter Park, Florida.

Sources for *Garrett's 1st Year*: papers by Hot Off the Press.

Sources for *A Merry Christmas*: spatter and snowflake papers by Provo Craft, dark polka dot paper by Carolee's Creations, plaid paper by Hot Off the Press.

Pages 10 – 11
Photos courtesy of Jennifer Pond, Highlands Ranch, Colorado.

Page 12
Photos by Diane Perry, 303.880.8481.
Sources for *Sunshine* Pages: various printed papers by Crafter's Workshop, Keeping Memories Alive, Lasting Impressions, The Paper Patch, Provo Craft, and Robin's Nest Press.

Page 13
Photos courtesy of Deborah Mock, Denver, Colorado.

Page 14
Sources for *Log Cabin* Quilt page: various printed papers by Carolee's Creations, DJ Inkers, E.K. Success, Ever After, Hot Off the Press, Karen Foster Design, Keeping Memories Alive, Northern Spy, The Paper Patch, and Provo Craft.

Page 34
Photos for peel and stick quilt page by Diane Gibbs, Richmond, Virginia.

Page 40
Sources for *Grandmother's Flower Garden* Quilt page: various printed papers by MiniGraphics, Northern Spy, The Paper Patch, and Provo Craft. Letter stickers by Frances Meyer. Pink button by Stampassions.

Page 52
Sources for *Tumbling Blocks* Quilt page: various printed papers by Hot Off the Press, Karen Foster Design, Keeping Memories Alive, Lasting Impressions, MiniGraphics, The Paper Patch, and Provo Craft.

Page 66
Sources for *Dresdan Plate* Quilt page: various printed papers by

Colors by Design, Frances Meyer, Hot Off the Press, Kangaroo & Joey, Northern Spy, NRN Designs, The Paper Adventures, and Paper Patch.

Page 70
Photos for *Wedding Ring* page by Sorensons Photography, 5331 SW Macadam, Portland, Oregon 97201, 503.223.3730.

Page 80
Photos for *Family Trees* by McBride Photography, 33 W First S., Rexburg, Idaho 83440, 208.356.5632.

Page 88
Sources for *Crazy Quilt* page: various plain and printed papers by Hot Off the Press, Keeping Memories Alive, Making Memories, Provo Craft, and Sonburn.

Page 96
Sources for *Spring 2000* Quilt page: printed papers by Northern Spy and Printworks.

Pages 120
Sources for "Love": template by Cut-It-Up

Sources for *"Quilt"*: paper by Current, stickers by Creative Memories. To make the outlined letters, cut thin outlines from the letter sticker "left-overs", adhere them to printed paper, and cut again.

Sources for *"Family"*: paper by MiniGraphics, template by Puzzlemates.

Calligraphy alphabet by Florence Davis, Winter Haven, Florida

Page 121
Sources for "Patchwork": Paper by Provo Craft and Paper Adventures, letter die cuts by Accu-Cut.

Manufacturers

The following companies manufacture products featured in this book. Please check your local retailers to find these materials. In addition, we have made every attempt to properly credit the trademarks and brand names of the items mentioned in this book. We apologize to any companies that have been listed incorrectly, and we would appreciate hearing from you.

Accu-Cut Systems ®
800.288-1670

All American Scrapbook Company 724.287.4311

All Night Media 800.782.6733

C&T Publishing 800.284.1114

Carolee's Creations 435.563.9336

ChartPak Crafts 800.628.1910

Classic Trio (Stens-a-Quilt) 714.526.5486

Close to My Heart 888.655.6552

Colors by Design 800.832.8436

Colorbök 800.366.4660 (wholesale only)

Conners Collectibles 800.995.6224

The Crafter's Workshop 877-crafter

Crafty Cutter 805.237.5834

Creative Imaginations 800.942.6487

Creative Memories® 800.468.9335

Current® 800.848.2848

Cut-It-Up™ 530.389.2233

DJ Inkers™ 800.944.4680

Design Originals 800.877.7820

E.K. Success™ (wholesale only) www.eksuccess.com

Ever After 800.646.0010

Family Treasures 800.413.2645

Fiskars®, Inc. 800.950.0203

Folded Memories 425.673.7422

Frances Meyer, Inc.® 800.372.6237

Geographics, Inc. 800.426.5923

The Gifted Line 800.533.7263

Grafix 800.447.2349

Guadalupe's Rubber Stamps 505.982.9862

Hallmark Cards, Inc. 800.halmark

Handmade Scraps, Inc. 877.915.1695

Hero Arts Rubber Stamps, Inc. 800.822.hero

Hot Off the Press® 800.227-9595

Inspire Graphics 877.grafics

Juliet Designs 800.848.7915

K & Company 888.244.2083

Kangaroo & Joey 800.646.8065

Karen Foster Design 801.451.9779

Keeping Memories Alive™ 800.947.3609

L Paper Designs 425.755.9636

Lasercraft, Inc. 800.358.8296

Lasting Impressions 800.9.emboss

Lighthouse Memories 909.879.0218

Magenta Art Rubberstamps & Accessories 800.565.5254

Making Memories 800.286.5263

Marvy Uchida 800.541.5877

McGill Inc. 800.982.9884

Memory Makers® magazine 800.366.6465

MiniGraphics 800.442.7035

MPR Associates, Inc. 800.454.3331

Mrs. Grossman's Paper Company 800.457.4570

My Mind's Eye™, Inc. 801.298.3709

Northern Spy 530.620.7430

NRN Designs (wholesale only) 800.421.6958

Pamela Shoy Papers 916.789.1025

Paper Adventures® 800.727.0699

The Paper Company 800.426.8989

The Paper Patch 801.253.3018 (wholesale only)

Pebbles in My Pocket® www.pebblesinmypocket.com

Personal Stamp Exchange 800.782.6748

Plaid Enterprises, Inc. 800.842.4197

PrintWorks 800.854.6558

Provo Craft® 800.937.7686

Puzzlemates 888.595.2887

RA Lang 800.648.2388

The Robin's Nest 435.789.5387

Rubber Stampede, Inc. 800.632.8386

Sonburn, Inc. 415.566.1018

Stamp Francisco 415.566.1018

Stampassions 800.art.stamp

Stampendous! 800.869.0474

StenSource® International, Inc. 800.642.9293

Stickapotamus® 888.270.4443

Wintech International 800.263.6043

Bibliography

Hall, Carrie A. and Rose G. Kretsinger. *The Romance of the Patchwork Quilt in America.* New York: Bonanza Books, 1935.

Ickis, Marguerite. *The Standard Book of Quilt Making and Collecting.* New York: Dover Press, 1959.

Linsley, Leslie. *America's Favorite Quilts.* New York: Delacorte Press, 1983.

Orlofsky, Patsy and Myron. *Quilts in America.* New York: Abbeville Press, Inc., 1992.

Soltow, Willow Ann. *Quilting the World Over.* Radnor, Pennsylvania: Chilton Book Company, 1991.

DETACH HERE